SELECTED POEMS OF

HENRY NEWBOLT

Henry Newbolt, 1889

SELECTED POEMS OF

HENRY NEWBOLT

Edited and with an Introduction
by
PATRIC DICKINSON

HODDER & STOUGHTON

LONDON SYDNEY AUCKLAND TORONTO

British Library Cataloguing in Publication Data
Newbolt, Sir Henry
 Selected Poems of Henry Newbolt.
 I. Title   II. Dickinson, Patric
 821'.912   PR5103.N4

ISBN 0 340 26388 1

Typography by Peter Newbolt. Printed in Great Britain for Hodder
& Stoughton Limited, Mill Road, Dunton Green, Sevenoaks, Kent by
St Edmundsbury Press, Bury St Edmunds, Suffolk. Typeset by Hewer
Text Composition Services.

Hodder & Stoughton Editorial Office: 47 Bedford Square,
London WC1B 3DP.

Acknowledgments

I would like to express my great gratitude to Peter Newbolt for all his co-operation, and for letting me have access to all the available notebooks and Mss. of his grandfather, which were of the greatest help in preparing this edition.

Also to Miss Aldington for her tireless diligence and efficiency in preparing the typescript.

P.D.

Contents

7

Henry Newbolt, 1862–1938

BY PATRIC DICKINSON

I

In 1911 Henry Newbolt published a 'Novel of Youth' called *The Twymans*. The first half of it is very largely autobiographical, and the first and vivid glimpse of Percival Twyman aged about six, is the first glimpse of Newbolt. He is painting. 'Oh, but it isn't a picture, it's Heraldry', he said with intense earnestness, 'and it's not red, it's gules, and you couldn't put brown on the lions, it would make them proper.' This may seem a pedantic remark for a little boy, but it is entirely in keeping with one side of Newbolt's character: his passion for accuracy. Indeed his lifelong pursuit of Heraldry does offer a key to his complex character. On one side is the controlled and logical demand for fact: an escutcheon must be correct, it must be true or nothing. His notebooks are full of heraldic drawings and genealogical tables. On the other side Heraldry opens a door upon a living past and the truth of the people behind the coats of arms, what they did and the ideals they stood for. The virtues of chivalry appealed immensely to the ardent simple and emotional side of Newbolt; he believed in them and celebrated them in whatever age he found them.

The two sides of his nature do not conflict, as one might expect, they are complementary and he was likely to have been aware of this in calling himself 'Percival Twyman'. Sir Percival (Wagner's Parsifal) is the nearest knight to fulfilling the Arthurian ideal, and 'Twyman' does suggest a duality. Whether this was conscious or not it is certainly true both of his life and of his work. He read with amusement what R. N. Bradley said of him in 1927 (*Racial Origins of the English Character*), 'We find in Newbolt the Nordic imbued with Mediterranean beauty.' In a memoir after his death his son-in-law, Sir Ralph Furse, refers to his having Jewish blood through his mother: 'It gave him a certain fire and impulsiveness and was responsible, I fancy, for his twin gift of poetry

11

and affairs.' Whatever was responsible he had gifts of a unique and remarkable kind.

Newbolt was born in Bilston, Staffordshire, where his father was vicar. The Newbolts, he remarked later, were not long-lived, for his father died at forty-two, and his grandfather at thirty-one. It was his father's second marriage, so he was a sadly unlucky man. Henry was only four when he died and Mrs Newbolt only twenty-eight. 'His mother', writes Furse, 'was a Stubbs and descended from a lady whose maiden name was Aaron and who married a Solomon.' Whatever she passed on to Henry, she herself had courage, selflessness, intelligence and pertinacity. She did not die until March 5th, 1921, having seen her son become a famous poet, man of letters, and man of affairs. It must have been odd for her to read *The Twymans* and see herself portrayed there. 'Some parts of this book are biographical', she notes on the flyleaf of a family copy. After Bilston the Newbolts moved to her parents in Walsall. Another Stubbs, Heath Stubbs, was the family solicitor.

When he was ten it was decided to send Henry to a preparatory boarding school at Caistor in Lincolnshire. Even for the 1870s it was old-fashioned and primitive, but it is obvious that Newbolt loved it, and the account of it he gives in *The Twymans* is not bettered in his autobiography. (In many ways it seems a life nearer to Wordsworth's at Hawkshead a hundred years before.) Newbolt looks out over the glooming flats, 'Tennyson's people'! Certainly this was the land where things were true. But the boys lived in an heroic present too. They eagerly awaited news of what was actually happening to Sir Garnet Wolseley's Ashanti expedition. Towards the end of his life Newbolt wrote, 'The Young of my generation had neither cruel experience nor dark apprehension to weaken them. We expected fighting and we prepared for it: but we felt as mighty as the heroes and heroines in a great saga and trusted ourselves to Destiny with incredible confidence'. These words refer to the time of the Jubilee of 1887 – yet further back too, for the Headmaster at Caistor would give them the news from Africa and go straight on with Vergil's *Aeneid* – perhaps the battle between the heroes Aeneas and Mezentius. (As a new boy at Clifton his master could not believe that Newbolt knew the poem so well that he could reel off an 'unseen' translation of any part in a flash, and accused him of cheating!) Both Sir Garnet and Aeneas were 'True'.

The Headmaster had a reputation for winning scholarships. There was a new school – it had been founded in 1862, the year of Newbolt's birth – at Bristol, called Clifton College. He advised Mrs Newbolt to enter Henry. He sat the scholarship exam at Clifton, and coming from the wilds of Lincolnshire his first glimpse of the Close was a vision to the little boy of an order and beauty which he says clearly he never forgot. He duly won a scholarship. Clifton took day-boys as well as boarders and Mrs Newbolt sensibly decided that it would be cheaper and pleasanter to keep the family together and move there. She took a house opposite the Close, so Henry slept in his own bed and never experienced the rigours of public school boarding. It could be argued therefore that he was hardly fitted to extol the system. On the other hand he played a full part in the life of the school, and since he could withdraw into privacy he was the more able to see what, at least for him, that life was. It had two different strands. The first was scholarship which in his time meant the teaching of Latin and Greek, and this teaching embraced the literature and culture of the ancient world. But it was more than a mere exercise to set a passage from *Lancelot and Elaine* into elegiac couplets. Tennyson was still alive. Faced with setting a piece of Keats, whom he did not know, he asked for the whole poem. His master lent him the whole of Keats, as a matter of course. Reading Classics was fruitful discipline but a private one. The other lesson he learned at Clifton was a public one. Newbolt did not suddenly invent or discover the 'public school spirit'. What he found was that the ideals of chivalry (of which he was already aware): service, self-sacrifice, courage, justice, and an attitude to good and evil based on the Christian ethic, were being propagated as the contemporary way to live. Naturally the most potent exponent of these ideals was the Headmaster in the Chapel pulpit. They are good ideals. All his life Newbolt believed them to be vital and lived by them. The debasement of the phrase 'playing the game' does not invalidate its proper meaning. To Newbolt there was no mystique about team-games; in fact he was neither a keen cricketer nor footballer. He was a runner – he won the school quarter-mile – and a rifle shot: another manifestation of his love of accuracy. Within a decade Clifton produced besides Newbolt men as distinguished and different as Francis

13

Younghusband, Douglas Haig, the philosopher McTaggart, Arthur Quiller-Couch and Roger Fry, all of whom, even Q, represent some chivalric virtue. The account of Percival Twyman at 'Downton' is warm and accurate. Another reason for the 'Percival' perhaps is that the Headmaster of Clifton was Dr Percival.

By the time he won a classical scholarship to Corpus Christi College, Oxford, in 1881, Newbolt was already writing poetry, Arthurian in matter and Tennysonian in manner. He went up to Oxford, one may say, with a somewhat complicated coat of arms, a real pedigree of learning and a rather contradictory motto: *Quid volo nisi ut ardeat* which was to be a favourite for life. 'What (sort of thing) do I wish for, save that it (may) take fire'. At the university he led an idyllic life, 'one long summer term'. He got his First in Honour Mods but failed to in Greats (owing to feuding between his tutor and the examiners, so his tutor thought). Certainly he had a first-class mind. In his second year he finished his long Arthurian poem, *A Fair Death*.

He made many friends. Anthony Hope Hawkins, F. S. Boas, his tutor Arthur Sidgwick, were lifelong. He dabbled in Liberal politics, spoke forthrightly at the Union, and became involved in a row over the election of its officers.

It is at Oxford that Percival Twyman and Henry Newbolt part company. After coming down, he turned to the Bar, and his career there, as one might suspect, was academic. 'Wait a bit,' said a judge to him years later, '. . . you think you are famous for your poems, and so you may be, but what has given you *immortality* is your work on the Law Digest.' It *was* a work! 20,000 legal decisions on 'Will' alone, codified to make a coherent articulated sequence. During his early unmarried days in London in the 1880s, Newbolt worked with ardour in East End boys' clubs and fully comprehended both his and the boys' side of the scales. But he also occupied himself with a remarkable and curious literary investigation. The meticulous side of his intellect was almost obsessive. (He would always count the exact number of words in an article, for instance: not 1,000 but 987.) He engaged himself in analysing plays and poems – a scene from *Lear*, say – in a particular way. He would count the lines, and the words in a line, in the scene, and note how the pattern of strict iambic was broken, how often it was broken in the same way, or in different ways, and so on. He did this too

14

with established poems such as a Keats ode or with poems contemporary to him. These metrical variations were allotted Greek letters and set out in patterns like cryptograms which fill pages of notebooks. Bridges' 'Whither O Splendid Ship' looks fascinating, but really these explorations are pointless to anyone but Newbolt – for him they were of extreme value. By this minutely laborious means he somehow aroused in himself an exquisite sense of rhythm and a very sharp ear which, when he came to write his own poetry, gave to it its unique blend of artistic subtlety and the speaking voice.

During the 'legal' decade between leaving Oxford and his first astonishing success, Newbolt married Margaret Duckworth whose father was squire at Orchardleigh, near Wells in Somerset. In those days, one could engage whole carriages on trains, and a large party of Newbolts and their friends the Chiltons were en route for a holiday at Lynton in North Devon. A guest was to be picked up at Yeovil. Margaret Duckworth boarded the train. She was beautiful, aloof, intelligent. Henry Newbolt fell entirely in love with her. It took nearly two years of negotiation and machination by all sorts of relatives – and another stop at Yeovil – before their marriage, which brought them lifelong happiness, a son, Francis, and a daughter, Celia, who married Ralph Furse. Margaret added to their circle her cousin Ella Coltman and her friend the poet Mary E. Coleridge. These two led Newbolt nearer to literature. They wrote serial romantic novels, a chapter each, and Newbolt his own verses very inferior to Mary's. So far he seems to have had no exact ambition. But having read Malory, *after* having read Tennyson's *Idylls of the King*, he was so disillusioned and incensed at the Laureate's bowdlerising and sheer cheating over the original that he wrote a five-act tragedy in blank verse called *Mordred* to establish the truth of the matter. This is typical of him. He nowhere says how, at the same time, he began writing poems and ballads about unimpeachable and verifiable heroes. But it seems reasonable to suppose that as one side of him was refuting a bogus hero Arthur, the other side was eagerly seeking true ones. Newbolt was born with a very strong sense of the past, an instinct for history. This was concentrated upon mediaeval history, and upon British colonial history of the eighteenth and nineteenth centuries; not in the generalities of politics, but in the single crystallised deeds of individuals. He went to astonishing lengths to find

15

his facts, although it would not be apparent from the ballad 'Craven' that he knew the exact design of the monitor *Tecumseh*, nor the disposition of the other ships in the battle. He consulted many papers and parish registers to verify the enchanting story of 'Fidele's Grassy Tomb', but all the pedantry and fastidiousness of one side of his nature would go for nothing were it not outweighed by his simple ardent nature as a poet. He had a particular gift for presenting his heroes in some climax, whether of action or decision, some life-and-death moment, as warm living individuals. Yet at the same time each is a symbol and embodies the values in which the poet believed – his genius lies in his never obtruding nor presenting a cause or case. He is almost as anonymous as a ballad singer and his presence or essence in a poem is purely benevolent to the poem. 'The Death of Admiral Blake' is a lyric unadulterated by any trace of false emotion. It follows that though the ballads concern historical figures it is not really necessary to know who they are, for the action and emotion have been commingled and distilled to produce poems which are entirely enjoyable in terms of the poet's art and only secondarily in terms of history.

It is in keeping that Newbolt should have been given his 'start' by Robert Bridges, an academic and opinionated poet, as unlike Newbolt as one could imagine. Luckily both were Classical scholars of Corpus, although Bridges was nearly twenty years senior.

When they first met in 1895 Newbolt was thirty-three. He and his wife had gone down to Yattendon to stay with Mrs Bridges' parents. Robert and his wife also lived in the village; they met at dinner. Newbolt stood up for himself and Bridges took to him.

The hold Classics had on education was beginning to weaken and Bridges had evolved an intricate system of rules for English prosody, equivalent to the rules for classical metre. Newbolt held his own in argument for he was the better scholar, and as to English he had made his own researches and did not in the least mind Bridges telling him he wrote by ear and not by rule. Mary Coleridge, another protégée of Bridges, spoke of an evening when he translated Newbolt's 'A Ballad of John Nicholson' into sprung rhythm and a bit of Hopkins into ballad form: the poems Newbolt showed Bridges at their first meeting were enough to convince him that Newbolt was a poet. Bridges set about showing them to Laurence Binyon who was editing a series of poetry pamphlets, *Elkin Mathews' Shilling Garland*. *Admirals All* had, appropriately enough, twelve poems in it. Eight were ballads, four were 'conventional' lyrics, but all of them had a quality that had been lost to English poetry. They were, above all, speakable and not literary, spontaneous and not calculated in precious words.

Timing is often important in a poet's career. In 1893 Kipling's colloquial *Barrack-Room Ballads* had attracted many by their realism and their strong and insistent rhythm. There is certainly nothing subtle about them. Moreover, soldiers of the Queen were always in fact battling on the edge of the Indian Empire. Kipling's gift was for immediate descriptions and special pleading for Tommy: for an opportunist and journalistic approach. Gunga Din is not a great man; he is merely in time and place a 'better' man. In these poems Kipling's underlying ideals seem crude and concerned with a warlike patriotism which is not to be confused with love of country. A further distinction from Newbolt is that while the army was real and active, the navy, being all powerful, never had to do anything and was a mystery. There is a corollary to this. Kipling started off as a spokesman for an actual contemporary army, but in the Edwardian decade became less and less so: Newbolt started off as the spokesman for an ideal and heroic navy, but he moved steadily into the counsels of the Admiralty which made him in time more or less an expert lay consultant on current naval affairs. The two writers were bound to be compared and when *Admirals All* came out in 1897, one Cambridge don remarked, in praise, that it was 'Kipling without the brutality'. It's hard to see why Newbolt was pleased, for the little book in its 'sugar paper' coloured covers was far more than that and it was recognised to be so, both for its underlying values as for its obviously attractive surface. Newbolt's own words are the best comment on the text. 'Between 1895–1900 Rudyard Kipling, Alfred Housman, and Henry Newbolt had secured an abundant harvest of popularity by sowing their wild oats – poems of vivid sentiment in vivid metre, by which each in his own way expressed the simplicity and spirit of his themes. This kind of poetry does not ordinarily work any change in the theory or practice of contemporary poets; being by its origin sincere it cannot be successfully imitated or followed in any way. Its only interest from a technical point of view, is that it is a set-off to too much theorising on the principles of literature. . . .' Newbolt's 'attack'

on Kipling was not on poetical, but political, grounds. They corres-
ponded but did not meet.

William Archer, translator of Ibsen, and the dramatic critic of his
time, gave Newbolt a wonderful notice. He recognised how Newbolt's
dramatic gift was perfectly employed in writing the impersonal ballad.
W. B. Yeats, whom he had first met at the Bridges', wrote in 1902 what
applies in general to *Admirals All*, *The Island Race* and *The Sailing of the
Long Ships*: 'You have said many wise and true and beautiful things in
rhyme. Yours is patriotism of the fine sort – patriotism that lays
burdens on a man, and not the patriotism that takes burdens off.' In
1897 Newbolt – aged thirty-five – became, at once, an astounding
success. Twenty-one editions of *Admirals All*, of a thousand copies
each, were sold in a year. Newbolt left the Bar. He decided he could
risk being a writer – and on the strength of *Admirals All* he got a
commission to do something he really wanted to do – his own version of
Froissart, which was published in 1900.

II

The period 1892–1909 was the most productive of Newbolt's life both in
poetry and prose. The three successive volumes filled out his repu-
tation and this is lucky for a poet in his lifetime for it was a deserved
reputation and not merely a fashionable and ephemeral success such
as attended Stephen Phillips. The immediate fame of poems such as
'Drake's Drum' put Newbolt's other poems at a disadvantage. His
lyrics are not divorced from the ballads – all are part of the same poet,
as are his very original light poems. Simply, the lyrics unjustly suffer
because they are not heroic. Any poet would have been glad to have
written 'Amore Altiero' or 'The Invasion', or 'Rilloby-Rill'. One must
judge any poet by his best work, but it is hard not to ignore the rest
when a very few pieces achieve a kind of over-fame which puts other
work into an exaggerated shade. The lyrics have their own qualities of
rhythm and a classical delicacy and restraint, as ever combined with
Newbolt's especial directness and zest. He was so much more than a
'mere ballad-monger', as he once described himself.

He was a smallish spare man, with a handsome ascetic face, rather
Roman-Imperatorial, and he had a thin precise tenor voice: (it can be

heard on old 78 recordings). To go with this he had what he called a
'sanguine' and others called a warm and delightful personality. The
success of *Admirals All* made him eager to make his mark. 'I had also
felt a hankering after some more direct form of communication, some
kind of literary and social journalism.' John Murray, the publisher,
invited him to edit a new literary monthly: 'to no one would we entrust
the editorship more readily than to yourself; for the position you have
won in the world of letters, coupled with your own personality, will
go far. . . .' There is no doubt that all his life Newbolt made friends
rather than enemies and that his charm, earnestness (*gravitas*), and
dependability made him an almost ideal choice for this venture.

The first number of *The Monthly Review* appeared in October 1900.
Newbolt was naturally disposed to give plenty of space to poetry and it
was not long before an unknown poet submitted some Mss. Newbolt at
once recognised the worth of 'Walter Ramal' and made it his business
to discover who he was: he discovered Walter de la Mare. Newbolt was
a practical man. He was convinced of de la Mare's genius, even before
he began to love him as a friend, so he engineered his escape from the
drudgery of being a clerk in the Rockefeller Standard Oil Trust. He
had the ear of the Prime Minister's private secretary, but Mr Asquith
had the awful example of Tennyson in front of him – Tennyson granted
a Civil List pension in his thirties and drawing it for over fifty years . . .
no, there could be no repetition of that. However, a lump sum from the
King's Bounty was available. Newbolt invested it shrewdly for him and
set de la Mare free.

Their friendship was lifelong and is the first instance of Newbolt's
quite remarkable gift, untainted by jealousy, for furthering what he
thought was new and good. He was able to hail Hardy's *The Dynasts*, at
once, as a masterpiece when the complete work was published in 1908.
Hardy was delighted, especially that a *poet* should feel like this. He
liked, 'Mr H. having decided on a chronicle play had to provide for it a
theatre under his own management', and various other acute criticisms.
(Hardy and Newbolt used to have long conversations at the Savile
Club.) The contents table of *The Monthly Review* are a fascinating mix-
ture of names, once familiar, still familiar or now forgotten. The ten first
pages to Walter Ramal, and in a later number, ten more to Walter de la
Mare, ten to the forgotten Lascelles Abercrombie . . . Roger Fry . . .

Anthony Hope . . . it was indeed a branching out for Newbolt. During this time he became a close friend of H. G. Wells, as their letters show, and indeed there were few people in the literary scene who did not know Henry Newbolt. Later in the decade he revived the moribund Royal Society of Literature and gave brilliant critical lectures there. He was one of the first critics to give encouragement to the 'new' poetry of Rupert Brooke in 1911 and of his 'Georgian' confrères.

1905 was the centenary of the battle of Trafalgar. Newbolt wrote an account of it. 'I doubt if I ever enjoyed any single piece of work so much as I enjoyed this.' His researches led him to believe that the official Admiralty account of the battle was wrong. He published his own account in the autumn, and it was so brilliantly convincing that within two years the navy had admitted it and acquired it as the truth of the matter. In doing so they acquired Newbolt too. Other researches into the past led Newbolt to the writing of two historical novels. *The Old Country* is a detailed exploration into the past of his wife's family and involves a present character being projected into the past (he later thought Henry James had stolen his ideas in his last unfinished book *The Sense of the Past*). *The New June* is a detailed re-creation of the time of Richard II. All the events are historically true but he chose to have his characters speak in natural Edwardian English according to their class. Both books in their day were great successes. There is a Clarendon Press edition of Shakespeare's *Richard II* with an introduction by Newbolt which any producer of the play could look at with advantage.

But what John Murray had not reckoned upon, when appointing Newbolt to the editorship of *The Monthly Review*, were his political aspirations. On coming down from Oxford he had set up for himself a 'parliament fund' in case he should ever be able to afford to stand. He was a dedicated Liberal and during the four years, 1900–1904, he propagated Liberal policies in Editorials and articles which filled the Tory Murray with the gravest alarm. He sacked Newbolt in August 1904, but by this time Newbolt had established himself as a political figure. His friendship with Sir Edward Grey (Lord Grey of Falloden) led him into the most intimate counsels of the party; he would meet Grey in the dedans of the tennis court at Lords on his way to the House to discuss secret policy in opposition, and when in power an untimely letter of Newbolt's to *The Times* nearly split the party and jeopardised their friendship. 'Mr Newbolt's Plan for Ireland' also published in *The Times* was given great prominence and earned a cartoon by Max, and indeed, photographed walking to No. 10 with Grey, he was once wrongly captioned as a Cabinet Minister.

He quite legitimately used *The Monthly Review* too, to print articles on naval affairs. These were mostly written by experts such as Bellairs and Corbett, but it was plain to the Admiralty that in Newbolt they had a knowledgeable and passionate supporter of the navy. His book on Trafalgar was added proof (it was mostly written while electioneering for his friend Josiah Wedgwood). So with Grey at the Foreign Office, the Liberals in power and the Admiralty open to him, Newbolt had a foot firmly in politics. 'As to the Foreign Secretary, he harps on my "gift for feeling and expression". If he had it he says he would have left politics years ago and written . . . poetry. I assured him that "expression" is not a gift of words but an effort of creation and painful. Would a man go on with it if not compelled to?'

In 1908 Admiral Sir Reginald Custance invited Newbolt to go on a week's cruise with the Channel Fleet. It was a recognition of the Newbolt who represented Drake and Hawke, and Nelson, and Duncan and the *Fighting Téméraire*, the Old *Superb*, the Bright *Medusa*, and Messmates: a recognition, too, of Newbolt and the modern navy, for as the Edwardian decade moved on there was no doubt in the minds of intelligent naval men that,

> Some day we're bound to sight the enemy,
> He's coming, tho' he hasn't yet a name . . .

Songs of the Fleet which sprang from this voyage, were poems Newbolt was 'compelled' to, and revelled in being compelled to, and as ever, these simple and glowing lyrics spring out of his having been shown all the technical workings, to the most secret, of a modern dreadnought. Indeed so deeply involved in the navy was he that Admiral ('Jackie') Fisher thought it worth having him spied upon, though they were good enough friends.

In 1909 Newbolt had published *Songs of Memory and Hope* the final culling of his first and most productive period. The poems are elegant and attractive, but backward-looking, and he admitted it. The six

Songs of the Fleet are a marvellous revival and culmination of his first inspiration. 'The Middle Watch' is perhaps the most perfect poem he ever wrote. The *Song*s were first published, as songs, with settings by Charles Villiers Stanford in 1910. They appeared as poems, in 1912, in his 'collected' *Poems: New and Old*. The very appearance of this collection shows how anxious Newbolt was to finish with his past and find a new style. 'I maintained to Hardy that a man cannot remain to the end of his career what he was at the beginning: ripeness is all, and the best that can happen is that a writer's work should always be changing for the riper, by a natural and not an artificial process.'

But though these thoughts were in his mind, he expended too much of his time in public affairs to realise them. It was a period when society was close-knit, and many discussions of importance took place at clubs such as the Athenaeum and over private dinner-tables. It was at one such dinner party in 1913 (at which Henry James was a fellow guest) that Mr Asquith offered Newbolt a Knighthood, which he accepted.

III

Many people are apt to look at the First World War backwards, as 1918–14. This is reasonable, for the particularly horrible nature of it was not manifest till 1916. Add to that, the poetry and prose which came out of it deal with the latter half, in revolt and disgust. It is somehow assumed that Brooke was a fool to write the 1914 sonnets, because he should have divined what the war was going to be like. Consequently the idea of patriotism or of a cause is subtly denigrated. That the youth of England *was* on fire, and moved by those virtues of chivalry which Newbolt so deeply believed in is a fact scamped by hindsight historians, but there is no reason to disbelieve it. In an editorial in *The Monthly Review* for February 1902, Newbolt had written: 'War, like life itself, is a game or else a brutality worse than bestial. If its immediate objects are paramount, all is over with the soul of man . . .' In a letter dated November 5th, 1918, he wrote '. . . I have come to believe that the best thing we can do is to kill the accursed and that isn't a job to rejoice over. To win a game makes the pulses leap but not to massacre – that only chokes and disgusts.' The word 'game' to Newbolt stood for a proper way of life with proper rules. He was fifty-two in 1914. To him and to many others the war which they knew was inevitable nevertheless came as a shock, because 'the immediate objects' of the Germans were paramount. They broke the rules of chivalry (the invasion of neutral Belgium, the sinking by U-boat of the *Lusitania*); and no less than the soul of man was at stake. 'Kill the accursed.' Between 1914–1918 Newbolt never wavered in his belief that the Germans were evil and that the war was a kind of Crusade. As always his mind went to basic principles and for a man of his age his view was perfectly tenable. But Newbolt was a complex personality: he had been for some time before 1914 dissatisfied with his style and had been meditating how to change it. To put it flatly, the war stifled him as an artist, and he knew it. He knew what would be expected of him. Perhaps the way to 'do' the war, he thought, was ballads, but he no longer wanted to write ballads, and as the war settled down there were no symbolic heroes. He managed to find one in the early days – Tom Bridges (see note on 'The Toy Band') – and wrote a splendid ballad; and later the destruction of the crafty German raider *Emden* by H.M.A.S. *Sydney* led to another, but really he was stuck fast in the spirit of 'St George's Day' and 'The Vigil' (see note). Naturally there was service: first in the Admiralty and then in Beaverbrook's Ministry of Information. It is typical of one side of his nature that he should have argued against Grey's general desire for peace, that *first* it was necessary to find a practical and successful counter to the U-Boat. 'Who won the war? A young man you never heard of !' This was Maurice Hankey, father of General Tank and Admiral Convoy! He was secretary to Lloyd George and got through his concept of convoy on April 30th, 1917. 'It was the turning point of the war.' Newbolt with his strategic sense was very quick to recognise this as a keypoint – but he could not write a ballad of Maurice Hankey. In 1918 he completely reverted to his worn-out style and wrote 'The Ballad of Sir Pertab Singh' (see note). It was not till the early twenties that he published his truest poem of the war and it is rightly called 'A Perpetual Memory, Good Friday 1915':

> Broken and pierced, hung on the bitter wire,
>   By their most precious death the Sons of Man
> Redeem for us the life of our desire –
>   O Christ how often since the world began !

23

But as *Admirals All* had changed his course from being only a poet to being a man of letters and affairs, so the war inevitably took him further away. By 1920 he had finished his own *Naval History of the War*, and hoped for 'nothing to do. That is the only hope of poems, the leisure and pleasure principle'. He was far from having nothing to do. In 1919 H. A. L. Fisher, President of the Board of Education had asked him to chair a report 'into the position of English in the educational systems'. He had distinguished members of the committee to support him such as his old friend F. S. Boas, Quiller-Couch, George Sampson, Caroline Spurgeon, and J. Dover Wilson. The report is masterly. There can be little doubt from an examination of the prose that finally Newbolt wrote most of it, if not all. Had it been implemented the teaching of English in schools would have been revolutionised. Fisher was delighted; but the report was shelved and there was a change of Government. But Newbolt believed that his service to his country still required more of him. When he was congratulated by Fisher he tentatively asked for a blessing on a proposed new series of English text books, and Fisher replied in Newboltian words that it would be 'the greatest service you could do for the country'. The series was suggested by his friend John Buchan – a man of the same cast of mind and spirit as Newbolt. Buchan was Educational Editor of the publisher Thomas Nelson, and the plan gave Newbolt a financial security which he needed, but it did not buy leisure. In 1922 his old friend from *The Monthly Review* days the naval historian Julian Corbett died, his official history of naval operations unfinished. Obviously Newbolt was the man to finish it, a four-year job, asked for in three. There are moments in his letters when he writes, 'I would like to write a hundred poems in a hundred days', or that he was writing poems all day and burying them at sunset, or that '. . . my real ambition is to leave some poems – enough of them to make a lasting change in men's ideas of Time and Eternity'. But there never was time. He wrote to Lady Newbolt in February 1927: 'It quite surprised me to find that you have been thinking this racketing time-wasting life is my ideal! I've made a firm stand against complaining, because I look at it as a necessary effort, like the War – a thing to be endured till we get what we thought worth fighting for.'

Throughout his life Newbolt had a passion for what was good in what was new, and not only in literature. He had been instrumental in saving from exploitation the young inventor Guglielmo Marconi (who was a cousin of Mary Coleridge's) when he came to England in 1896. During the war he had suggested to Beaverbrook the idea of a world network of Imperial wireless-news-stations – an idea approved of by everyone, but scotched by the Treasury. He broadcast for Reith talks on poetry which would grace Radio Three today – if he could get half-hours for them! In 1911 he had championed the 'new' poetry; after the war, though he was striving to find a new voice, he was extraordinarily alert to poets younger than himself. In 1927 he published an anthology, *New Paths on Helicon*, of thirty-eight poets, with a critical commentary on each – Eliot, Pound, Edith Sitwell, Herbert Read, D. H. Lawrence and Peter Quennell among them. They were 'notes' he wrote, 'on individual poets, their characteristics, subjects, technique, principles and method: with a consideration of the possible result of their work on the future of poetry and of thought'. The commentaries are acute and perceptive, and too concentrated fairly to quote from. A single sentence from his *Edward Thomas* must serve to convey their flavour. 'He loved his country – he did not so much inhabit England as haunt it'. It is a work of great vitality and it shows what a zest and love for poetry Newbolt quite impersonally had. He included five poems of his own of which two, 'The Linnet's Nest' and 'The Nightjar' are really new. They are – more's the pity – the only two of such poems about Time and Eternity as he hoped to leave. There is a hint of Bridges' narrative style but it was transmuted by Newbolt's humanity. His foot was just in the door, but at 65 (in 1927) there was too much, a world, in between. When Bridges died in 1930, he was mooted as Poet Laureate, but, as he said, he wouldn't have suited Ramsay Macdonald's politics or pacifist ethics. He was of the wrong generation. Anyway, he had been unofficial poet laureate, de facto, for most of his life, and what he had written was spontaneous, he simply could not now write to order. This is true of his poetry, but it is not true of his loyalty nor sense of occasion. The King's private secretary Lord Stamfordham asked him if he would write for George V his broadcast to the nation in 1935 on recovery from his illness at Bognor Regis. It was the first time a King had ever broadcast: the words were Newbolt's.

The wretched thing that Newbolt found was that he could not write poems to his *own* order. Quid volo nisi ut ardeat? 'The Linnet's Nest' and 'The Nightjar' hint at what he was striving to do, which was to find a style in which he could set free his own private spirit from too long a bondage to his public spirit. This was in no sense selfish: that it was too late is a private tragedy for him as an artist, but it does not detract one jot from all that as an artist he had achieved. It is worth recalling what 'the War' meant to the Irishman Yeats – a new patriotic stimulus from the heroes of 1916, while the aftermath belonged to a couple of ambitious expatriate Americans also uninvolved in it. It would have been a superhuman effort for Newbolt to recreate himself as a poet. As it was, he wrote a very few poems in the twenties. On the whole they are 'new' in that they are contemplative, gentle, and wise in mood, but they are not so new in style as he would have wished and they turn to the past, or to a present which is told in terms of birds rather than human beings, and once to a future which in human hands was likely to be disastrous. He fully foresaw the menace of Germany again and it filled him with despair. His last poem 'The Star in the West' was written, as all his life he had desired his poetry to be, to be listened to, to be spoken aloud. It is a Nativity in which men have murdered night, made stars of their own, and 'Peace has died by fire'. There can be few sadder poems in the context of a poet's life in any century.

Newbolt's values depended upon absolute trust. After the war there was no such trust as he knew left among men. All his values were in vacuo, he could only be sure of finding a heroic moment in a linnet on her nest, or a vision of the meaning of time in the death of a nightjar whose loveliness went:

> full fathom five
> To the soul's ocean cave, where Wonder and Reason
> Tell their alternate dreams of how the world was made.

Wonder and Reason were the poles of his genius and his personality. In the last three years of his life he was attacked by some undiagnosable nervous melancholic disease. 'He never lost his characteristically in-cisive way of expressing himself when spoken to, but he became more and more silent and withdrawn into himself', writes Lady Newbolt. Perhaps he was, simply, overcome by the contrast between the world he had come from and the world he had lived into. It is not wholly fanciful to suppose that the soul of this brilliant and singular man had itself withdrawn into its own ocean cave.

A Note on the Text

Before the appearance of *Admirals All* Newbolt had privately printed
A Fair Death; 'an Arthurian story of some length in rhyme royal of the
Morrisian style'; and a five-act blank verse tragedy *Mordred* (1895)
which he wrote, by his own account, largely to correct Tennyson's
misuse of Malory. He never attempted to reprint either. As late as
January 1925 he wrote, 'But I have (so far) resisted all temptations to
tinker *Mordred* and reprint it.' In either case one cannot dispute his
judgment. As to the published poems, he was a meticulous corrector of
drafts. As to tinkering: 'I have a strong feeling against it myself – it is
always very distasteful to me that any trace of tinkering should remain
in rough drafts. I always burn them when they are on loose sheets, and
obliterate changes when they are in Mss. books.' He was not a poet who
would have wished to have his 'work sheets' published. There are, in
the Mss., considered improvements which do not wholly obliterate what
went before, and none, it seems to me, is ill-considered. The texts of his
various books therefore present little difficulty. As to the posthumous
volume, *A Perpetual Memory* (1939), nearly all the poems were written
in the 1920s and many printed. The last, 'The Star in the West', was
written in November 1932 and appeared in the Christmas number of
The Listener. It is possible that Newbolt would not have printed the few
epitaphs and inscriptions, but they are very much in keeping with his
work and character, and the book was arranged by Lady Newbolt.

Apart from the early *Collected Poems, 1897–1907*, the nearest to a
'collected' Newbolt is *Poems: New and Old* which was first published in
1912 and went into many editions. It is the single volume by which he is
best known. Its disadvantage is that it is (loosely) arranged by subject
matter and is in no sense chronological. It is possible to date, from a
notebook, nearly three-quarters of Newbolt's poems by year, by month,
or by day or days, but for an overall view of his work it has seemed best,
in almost every instance, to select them volume by volume in the order
in which, in each volume, they originally appeared.

It is not necessary to cite the countless anthologies in which his work may be found, but four poems in the posthumous volume – 'The Great Memory', 'The Linnet's Nest', 'The Nightjar', and 'After Church' – and two from *St George's Day* he put into his own anthology *New Paths on Helicon* (Nelson, 1927). 'The Linnet's Nest' had been published as an Ariel Poem (Faber & Gwyer, 1924), and 'The Nativity', which is not here printed, under the title 'A Child is Born', in a limited edition of 200 copies (Faber and Faber, 1931).

Admirals All

Effingham, Grenville, Raleigh, Drake,
 Here's to the bold and free!
Benbow, Collingwood, Byron, Blake,
 Hail to the Kings of the Sea!
Admirals all, for England's sake,
 Honour be yours and fame!
And honour, as long as waves shall break,
 To Nelson's peerless name!

 Admirals all, for England's sake,
  Honour be yours and fame!
 And honour, as long as waves shall break,
  To Nelson's peerless name!

Essex was fretting in Cadiz Bay
 With the galleons fair in sight;
Howard at last must give him his way,
 And the word was passed to fight.
Never was schoolboy gayer than he,
 Since holidays first began:
He tossed his bonnet to wind and sea,
 And under the guns he ran.

Drake nor devil nor Spaniard feared,
 Their cities he put to the sack;
He singed his Catholic Majesty's beard,
 And harried his ships to wrack.
He was playing at Plymouth a rubber of bowls
 When the great Armada came;
But he said, 'They must wait their turn, good souls',
 And he stooped, and finished the game.

Fifteen sail were the Dutchmen bold,
    Duncan he had but two:
But he anchored them fast where the Texel shoaled
    And his colours aloft he flew.
'I've taken the depth to a fathom', he cried,
    'And I'll sink with a right good will,
For I know when we're all of us under the tide,
    My flag will be fluttering still.'

Splinters were flying above, below,
    When Nelson sailed the Sound:
'Mark you, I wouldn't be elsewhere now',
    Said he, 'for a thousand pound!'
The Admiral's signal bade him fly,
    But he wickedly wagged his head,
He clapped the glass to his sightless eye
    And 'I'm damned if I see it', he said.

Admirals all, they said their say
    (The echoes are ringing still),
Admirals all, they went their way
    To the haven under the hill.
But they left us a kingdom none can take,
    The realm of the circling sea,
To be ruled by the rightful sons of Blake
    And the Rodneys yet to be.

Admirals all, for England's sake,
    Honour be yours and fame!
And honour, as long as waves shall break,
    To Nelson's peerless name!

November, 1892

San Stefano

A BALLAD OF THE BOLD MENELAUS

It was morning at St Helen's, in the great and gallant days,
    And the sea beneath the sun glittered wide,
When the frigate set her courses, all a-shimmer in the haze,
    And she hauled her cable home and took the tide.
She'd a right fighting company, three hundred men and more,
    Nine and forty guns in tackle running free;
And they cheered her from the shore for her colours at the fore,
    When the bold *Menelaus* put to sea.

She'd a right fighting company, three hundred men and more,
    Nine and forty guns in tackle running free;
And they cheered her from the shore for her colours at the fore,
    When the bold Menelaus *put to sea.*

She was clear of Monte Cristo, she was heading for the land,
    When she spied a pennant red and white and blue;
They were foemen, and they knew it, and they'd half a league
      in hand,
    But she flung aloft her royals and she flew.
She was nearer, nearer, nearer, they were caught beyond a doubt,
    But they slipped her, into Orbetello Bay,
And the lubbers gave a shout as they paid their cables out,
    With the guns grinning round them where they lay.

Now Sir Peter was a captain of a famous fighting race,
    Son and grandson of an admiral was he;
And he looked upon the batteries, he looked upon the chase,
    And he heard the shout that echoed out to sea.
And he called across the decks, 'Ay! the cheering might be late
    If they kept it till the *Menelaus* runs;
Bid the master and his mate heave the lead and lay her straight
    For the prize lying yonder by the guns.'

When the summer moon was setting, into Orbetello Bay
    Came the *Menelaus* gliding like a ghost;
And her boats were manned in silence, and in silence pulled away,
    And in silence every gunner took his post.
With a volley from her broadside the citadel she woke,
    And they hammered back like heroes all the night;
But before the morning broke she had vanished through the smoke
    With her prize upon her quarter grappled tight.

It was evening at St Helen's, in the great and gallant time,
    And the sky behind the down was flushing far;
And the flags were all a-flutter, and the bells were all a-chime,
    When the frigate cast her anchor off the bar.
She'd a right fighting company, three hundred men and more,
    Nine and forty guns in tackle running free;
And they cheered her from the shore for her colours at the fore,
    When the bold *Menelaus* came from sea.

She'd a right fighting company, three hundred men and more,
    Nine and forty guns in tackle running free;
And they cheered her from the shore for her colours at the fore,
    When the bold Menelaus *came from sea.*

November, 1894

Drake's Drum

Drake he's in his hammock an' a thousand mile away,
    (Capten, art tha sleepin' there below?),
Slung atween the round shot in Nombre Dios Bay,
    An' dreamin' arl the time o' Plymouth Hoe.
Yarnder lumes the Island, yarnder lie the ships,
    Wi' sailor lads a-dancin' heel-an'-toe,
An' the shore-lights flashin', an' the night-tide dashin',
    He sees et arl so plainly as he saw et long ago.

Drake he was a Devon man, an' rüled the Devon seas,
    (Capten, art tha sleepin' there below?),
Rovin' tho' his death fell, he went wi' heart at ease,
    An' dreamin' arl the time o' Plymouth Hoe.
'Take my drum to England, hang et by the shore,
    Strike et when your powder's runnin' low;
If the Dons sight Devon, I'll quit the port o' Heaven,
    An' drum them up the Channel as we drummed them
        long ago.'

Drake he's in his hammock till the great Armadas come,
    (Capten, art tha sleepin' there below?),
Slung atween the round shot, listenin' for the drum,
    An' dreamin' arl the time o' Plymouth Hoe.
Call him on the deep sea, call him up the Sound,
    Call him when ye sail to meet the foe;
Where the old trade's plyin' an' the old flag flyin'
    They shall find him ware an' wakin', as they found him
        long ago!

December 5th, 1895

The Fighting Téméraire

It was eight bells ringing,
　For the morning watch was done,
And the gunner's lads were singing
　As they polished every gun.
It was eight bells ringing,
And the gunner's lads were singing,
For the ship she rode a-swinging
　As they polished every gun.

Oh! to see the linstock lighting,
*　Téméraire! Téméraire!*
Oh! to hear the round shot biting,
*　Téméraire! Téméraire!*
Oh! to see the linstock lighting,
And to hear the round shot biting,
For we're all in love with fighting
*　On the Fighting Téméraire.*

It was noontide ringing,
　And the battle just begun,
When the ship her way was winging
　As they loaded every gun.
It was noontide ringing,
When the ship her way was winging,
And the gunner's lads were singing
　As they loaded every gun.

There'll be many grim and gory,
*　Téméraire! Téméraire!*
There'll be few to tell the story,
*　Téméraire! Téméraire!*
There'll be many grim and gory,
There'll be few to tell the story,
But we'll all be one in glory
*　With the Fighting Téméraire.*

There's a far bell ringing
　　At the setting of the sun,
And a phantom voice is singing
　　Of the great days done.
There's a far bell ringing,
And a phantom voice is singing
Of renown for ever clinging
　　To the great days done.

　　Now the sunset breezes shiver,
　　　　Téméraire! Téméraire!
　　And she's fading down the river,
　　　　Téméraire! Téméraire!
　　Now the sunset breezes shiver,
　　And she's fading down the river,
　　But in England's song for ever
　　　　She's the Fighting Téméraire.

March 25th, 1897

Hawke

In seventeen hundred and fifty nine,
　　When Hawke came swooping from the West,
The French King's Admiral with twenty of the line,
　　Was sailing forth, to sack us, out of Brest.
The ports of France were crowded, the quays of France a-hum
With thirty thousand soldiers marching to the drum,
For bragging time was over and fighting time was come
　　When Hawke came swooping from the West.

'Twas long past noon of a wild November day
　　When Hawke came swooping from the West;
He heard the breakers thundering in Quiberon Bay,
　　But he flew the flag for battle, line abreast.

Down upon the quicksands roaring out of sight
Fiercely beat the storm-wind, darkly fell the night,
But they took the foe for pilot and the cannon's glare for light
  When Hawke came swooping from the West.

The Frenchmen turned like a covey down the wind
  When Hawke came swooping from the West;
One he sank with all hands, one he caught and pinned,
  And the shallows and the storm took the rest.
The guns that should have conquered us they rusted on the shore,
The men that would have mastered us they drummed and marched
    no more,
For England was England, and a mighty brood she bore
  When Hawke came swooping from the West.

March 19th–20th, 1897

Vitaï Lampada

There's a breathless hush in the Close to-night –
  Ten to make and the match to win –
A bumping pitch and a blinding light,
  An hour to play and the last man in.
And it's not for the sake of a ribboned coat,
  Or the selfish hope of a season's fame,
But his Captain's hand on his shoulder smote –
  'Play up! play up! and play the game!'

The sand of the desert is sodden red, –
  Red with the wreck of a square that broke; –
The Gatling's jammed and the Colonel dead,
  And the regiment blind with dust and smoke.

The river of death has brimmed his banks,
   And England's far, and Honour a name,
But the voice of a schoolboy rallies the ranks:
   'Play up! play up! and play the game!'

This is the word that year by year,
   While in her place the School is set,
Every one of her sons must hear,
   And none that hears it dare forget.
This they all with a joyful mind
   Bear through life like a torch in flame,
And falling fling to the host behind –
   'Play up! play up! and play the game!'

June, 1892

A Ballad of John Nicholson

It fell in the year of Mutiny,
   At darkest of the night,
John Nicholson by Jalándhar came,
   On his way to Delhi fight.

And as he by Jalándhar came
   He thought what he must do,
And he sent to the Rajah fair greeting,
   To try if he were true.

'God grant your Highness length of days,
   And friends when need shall be;
And I pray you send your Captains hither,
   That they may speak with me.'

39

On the morrow through Jalándhar town
    The Captains rode in state;
They came to the house of John Nicholson
    And stood before the gate.

The chief of them was Mehtab Singh,
    He was both proud and sly;
His turban gleamed with rubies red,
    He held his chin full high.

He marked his fellows how they put
    Their shoes from off their feet;
'Now wherefore make ye such ado
    These fallen lords to greet?

'They have ruled us for a hundred years,
    In truth I know not how,
But though they be fain of mastery,
    They dare not claim it now.'

Right haughtily before them all
    The durbar hall he trod,
With rubies red his turban gleamed,
    His feet with pride were shod.

They had not been an hour together,
    A scanty hour or so,
When Mehtab Singh rose in his place
    And turned about to go.

Then swiftly came John Nicholson
    Between the door and him,
With anger smouldering in his eyes
    That made the rubies dim.

'You are overhasty, Mehtab Singh,' –
  Oh, but his voice was low!
He held his wrath with a curb of iron,
  That furrowed cheek and brow.

'You are overhasty, Mehtab Singh,
  When that the rest are gone,
I have a word that may not wait
  To speak with you alone.'

The Captains passed in silence forth
  And stood the door behind;
To go before the game was played
  Be sure they had no mind.

But there within John Nicholson
  Turned him on Mehtab Singh,
'So long as the soul is in my body
  You shall not do this thing.

'Have ye served us for a hundred years
  And yet ye know not why?
We brook no doubt of our mastery,
  We rule until we die.

'Were I the one last Englishman
  Drawing the breath of life,
And you the master-rebel of all
  That stir this land to strife –

'Were I', he said, 'but a Corporal,
  And you a Rajput King,
So long as the soul was in my body
  You should not do this thing.

'Take off, take off those shoes of pride,
    Carry them whence they came;
Your Captains saw your insolence
    And they shall see your shame.'

When Mehtab Singh came to the door
    His shoes they burned his hand,
For there in long and silent lines
    He saw the Captains stand.

When Mehtab Singh rode from the gate
    His chin was on his breast:
The Captains said, 'When the strong command
    Obedience is best.'

The Guides at Cabul

1879

Sons of the Island Race, wherever ye dwell,
    Who speak of your fathers' battles with lips that burn,
The deed of an alien legion hear me tell,
    And think not shame from the hearts ye tamed to learn,
    When succour shall fail and the tide for a season turn,
To fight with a joyful courage, a passionate pride,
To die at the last as the Guides at Cabul died.

For a handful of seventy men in a barrack of mud,
    Foodless, waterless, dwindling one by one,
Answered a thousand yelling for English blood
    With stormy volleys that swept them gunner from gun,
    And charge on charge in the glare of the Afghan sun,
Till the walls were shattered wherein they crouched at bay,
And dead or dying half of the seventy lay.

Twice they had taken the cannon that wrecked their hold,
    Twice toiled in vain to drag it back,
Thrice they toiled, and alone, wary and bold,
    Whirling a hurricane sword to scatter the rack,
    Hamilton, last of the English, covered their track,
'Never give in!' he cried, and he heard them shout,
And grappled with death as a man that knows not doubt.

And the Guides looked down from their smouldering barrack again,
    And behold, a banner of truce, and a voice that spoke:
'Come, for we know that the English all are slain,
    We keep no feud with men of a kindred folk;
    Rejoice with us to be free of the conqueror's yoke.'
Silence fell for a moment, then was heard
A sound of laughter and scorn, and an answering word.

'Is it we or the lords we serve who have earned this wrong,
    That ye call us to flinch from the battle they bade us fight?
We that live – do ye doubt that our hands are strong?
    They that have fallen – ye know that their blood was bright!
    Think ye the Guides will barter for lust of the light
The pride of an ancient people in warfare bred,
Honour of comrades living, and faith to the dead?'

Then the joy that spurs the warrior's heart
    To the last thundering gallop and sheer leap
Came on the men of the Guides; they flung apart
    The doors not all their valour could longer keep;
    They dressed their slender line; they breathed deep,
And with never a foot lagging or head bent,
To the clash and clamour and dust of death they went.

November 21st–22nd, 1895

Ionicus

I live – I am old – I return to the ground –
Blow trumpets! and still I can dream to the sound.
William Cory

With failing feet and shoulders bowed
    Beneath the weight of happier days,
He lagged among the heedless crowd,
    Or crept along suburban ways.
But still through all his heart was young,
    His mood a joy that nought could mar,
A courage, a pride, a rapture, sprung
    Of the strength and splendour of England's war.

From ill-requited toil he turned
    To ride with Picton and with Pack,
Among his grammars inly burned
    To storm the Afghan mountain-track.
When midnight chimed, before Quebec
    He watched with Wolfe till the morning star;
At noon he saw from *Victory's* deck
    The sweep and splendour of England's war.

Beyond the book his teaching sped,
    He left on whom he taught the trace
Of kinship with the deathless dead,
    And faith in all the Island Race.
He passed; his life a tangle seemed,
    His age from fame and power was far;
But his heart was high to the end, and dreamed
    Of the sound and splendour of England's war.

January 22nd–23rd, 1896

Minora Sidera

Sitting at times over a hearth that burns
   With dull domestic glow,
My thought, leaving the book, gratefully turns
   To you who planned it so.

Not of the great only you deigned to tell –
   The stars by which we steer –
But lights out of the night that flashed, and fell
   To night again, are here.

Such as were those, dogs of an elder day,
   Who sacked the golden ports,
And those later who dared grapple their prey
   Beneath the harbour forts:

Some with flag at the fore, sweeping the world
   To find an equal fight,
And some who joined war to their trade, and hurled
   Ships of the line in flight.

Whether their fame centuries long should ring
   They cared not over-much,
But cared greatly to serve God and the king,
   And keep the Nelson touch;

And fought to build Britain above the tide
   Of wars and windy fate;
And passed content, leaving to us the pride
   Of lives obscurely great.

April 28th, 1896

Laudabunt Alii

(AFTER HORACE)

Let others praise, as fancy wills,
   Berlin beneath her trees,
Or Rome upon her seven hills,
   Or Venice by her seas;
Stamboul by double tides embraced,
Or green Damascus in the waste.

For me there's nought I would not leave
   For the good Devon land,
Whose orchards down the echoing cleeve
   Bedewed with spray-drift stand,
And hardly bear the red fruit up
That shall be next year's cider-cup.

You too, my friend, may wisely mark
   How clear skies follow rain,
And lingering in your own green park
   Or drilled on Laffan's Plain,
Forget not with the festal bowl
To soothe at times your weary soul.

When Drake must bid to Plymouth Hoe
   Good-bye for many a day,
And some were sad that feared to go,
   And some that dared not stay,
Be sure he bade them broach the best
And raised his tankard with the rest.

'Drake's luck to all that sail with Drake
   For promised lands of gold!
Brave lads, whatever storms may break,
   We've weathered worse of old!
To-night the loving-cup we'll drain,
To-morrow for the Spanish Main!'

August 17th, 1895

The Vigil

England! where the sacred flame
　　Burns before the inmost shrine,
Where the lips that love thy name
　　Consecrate their hopes and thine,
Where the banners of thy dead
Weave their shadows overhead,
Watch beside thine arms to-night,
Pray that God defend the Right.

Think that when to-morrow comes
　　War shall claim command of all,
Thou must hear the roll of drums,
　　Thou must hear the trumpet's call.
Now, before they silence ruth,
Commune with the voice of truth;
England! on thy knees to-night
Pray that God defend the Right.

Hast thou counted up the cost,
　　What to foeman, what to friend?
Glory sought is Honour lost,
　　How should this be knighthood's end?
Know'st thou what is Hatred's meed?
What the surest gain of Greed?
England! wilt thou dare to-night
Pray that God defend the Right?

Single-hearted, unafraid,
　　Hither all thy heroes came,
On this altar's steps were laid
　　Gordon's life and Outram's fame.
England! if thy will be yet
By their great example set,
Here beside thine arms to-night
Pray that God defend the Right.

So shalt thou when morning comes
 Rise to conquer or to fall,
Joyful hear the rolling drums,
 Joyful hear the trumpets call.
Then let Memory tell thy heart;
'England! what thou wert, thou art!'
Gird thee with thine ancient might,
Forth! and God defend the Right!

    December 18th, 1897

Admiral Death

Boys, are ye calling a toast to-night?
 (Hear what the sea-wind saith)
Fill for a bumper strong and bright,
 And here's to Admiral Death!
He's sailed in a hundred builds o' boat,
He's fought in a thousand kinds o' coat,
He's the senior flag of all that float,
 And his name's Admiral Death.

Which of you looks for a service free?
 (Hear what the sea-wind saith)
The rules o' the service are but three
 When ye sail with Admiral Death.
Steady your hand in time o' squalls,
Stand to the last by him that falls,
And answer clear to the voice that calls,
 'Ay, ay! Admiral Death!'

How will ye know him among the rest?
 (Hear what the sea-wind saith)
By the glint o' the stars that cover his breast
 Ye may find Admiral Death.

48

By the forehead grim with an ancient scar,
By the voice that rolls like thunder far,
By the tenderest eyes of all that are,
    Ye may know Admiral Death.

Where are the lads that sailed before?
    (Hear what the sea-wind saith)
Their bones are white by many a shore,
    They sleep with Admiral Death.
Oh! but they loved him, young and old,
For he left the laggard, and took the bold,
And the fight was fought, and the story's told,
    And they sleep with Admiral Death.

The Quarter-Gunner's Yarn

We lay at St Helen's, and easy she rode
With one anchor catted and fresh-water stowed;
When the barge came alongside like bullocks we roared,
For we knew what we carried with Nelson aboard.

Our Captain was Hardy, the pride of us all,
I'll ask for none better when danger shall call;
He was hardy by nature and Hardy by name,
And soon by his conduct to honour he came.

The third day the Lizard was under our lee,
Where the *Ajax* and *Thunderer* joined us at sea,
But what with foul weather and tacking about,
When we sighted the Fleet we were thirteen days out.

The Captains they all came aboard quick enough,
But the news that they brought was as heavy as duff;
So backward an enemy never was seen,
They were harder to come at than Cheeks the Marine.

49

The lubbers had hare's lugs where seamen have ears,
So we stowed all saluting and smothered our cheers,
And to humour their stomachs and tempt them to dine,
In the offing we showed them but six of the line.

One morning the topmen reported below
The old *Agamemnon* escaped from the foe.
Says Nelson: 'My lads, there'll be honour for some,
For we're sure of a battle now Berry has come.'

'Up hammocks!' at last cried the bo'sun at dawn;
The guns were cast loose and the tompions drawn;
The gunner was bustling the shot racks to fill,
And 'All hands to quarters!' was piped with a will.

We now saw the enemy bearing ahead,
And to East of them Cape Traflagar it was said,
'Tis a name we remember from father to son,
That the days of old England may never be done.

The *Victory* led, to her flag it was due,
Tho' the *Téméraires* thought themselves Admirals too;
But Lord Nelson he hailed them with masterful grace:
'Cap'n Harvey, I'll thank you to keep in your place.'

To begin with we closed the *Bucentaure* alone,
An eighty-gun ship and their Admiral's own;
We raked her but once, and the rest of the day
Like a hospital hulk on the water she lay.

To our battering next the *Redoutable* struck,
But her sharpshooters gave us the worst of the luck:
Lord Nelson was wounded, most cruel to tell,
'They've done for me, Hardy!' he cried as he fell.

To the cockpit in silence they carried him past,
And sad were the looks that were after him cast;
His face with a kerchief he tried to conceal,
But we knew him too well from the truck to the keel.

When the Captain reported a victory won,
'Thank God!' he kept saying, 'my duty I've done.'
At last came the moment to kiss him good-bye,
And the Captain for once had the salt in his eye.

'Now anchor, dear Hardy', the Admiral cried;
But before we could make it he fainted and died.
All night in the trough of the sea we were tossed,
And for want of ground-tackle good prizes were lost.

Then we hauled down the flag, at the fore it was red,
And blue at the mizzen was hoisted instead
By Nelson's famed Captain, the pride of each tar,
Who fought in the *Victory* off Cape Traflagar.

April 2nd–4th, 1898

For a Trafalgar Cenotaph

Lover of England, stand awhile and gaze
With thankful heart, and lips refrained from praise;
They rest beyond the speech of human pride
Who served with Nelson and with Nelson died.

Craven

MOBILE BAY, 1864

Over the turret, shut in his iron-clad tower,
    Craven was conning his ship through smoke and flame;
Gun to gun he had battered the fort for an hour,
    Now was the time for a charge to end the game.

There lay the narrowing channel, smooth and grim,
　　A hundred deaths beneath it, and never a sign;
There lay the enemy's ships, and sink or swim
　　The flag was flying, and he was head of the line.

The fleet behind was jamming; the monitor hung
　　Beating the stream; the roar for a moment hushed;
Craven spoke to the pilot; slow she swung;
　　Again he spoke, and right for the foe she rushed.

Into the narrowing channel, between the shore
　　And the sunk torpedoes lying in treacherous rank;
She turned but a yard too short; a muffled roar,
　　A mountainous wave, and she rolled, righted, and sank.

Over the manhole, up in the iron-clad tower,
　　Pilot and Captain met as they turned to fly:
The hundredth part of a moment seemed an hour,
　　For one could pass to be saved, and one must die.

They stood like men in a dream: Craven spoke,
　　Spoke as he lived and fought, with a Captain's pride,
'After you, Pilot': the pilot woke,
　　Down the ladder he went, and Craven died.

All men praise the deed and the manner, but we –
　　We set it apart from the pride that stoops to the proud,
The strength that is supple to serve the strong and free,
　　The grace of the empty hands and promises loud:

Sidney thirsting a humbler need to slake,
　　Nelson waiting his turn for the surgeon's hand,
Lucas crushed with chains for a comrade's sake,
　　Outram coveting right before command,

These were paladins, these were Craven's peers,
　　These with him shall be crowned in story and song,
Crowned with the glitter of steel and the glimmer of tears,
　　Princes of courtesy, merciful, proud and strong.

Messmates

He gave us all a good-bye cheerily
    At the first dawn of day;
We dropped him down the side full drearily
    When the light died away.
It's a dead dark watch that he's a-keeping there,
And a long, long night that lags a-creeping there,
Where the Trades and the tides roll over him
    And the great ships go by.

He's there alone with green seas rocking him
    For a thousand miles round;
He's there alone with dumb things mocking him,
    And we're homeward bound.
It's a long, lone watch that he's a-keeping there,
And a dead cold night that lags a-creeping there,
While the months and the years roll over him
    And the great ships go by.

I wonder if the tramps come near enough
    As they thrash to and fro,
And the battle-ships' bells ring clear enough
    To be heard down below;
If through all the lone watch that he's a-keeping there,
And the long, cold night that lags a-creeping there,
The voices of the sailor-men shall comfort him
    When the great ships go by.

The Death of Admiral Blake

AUGUST 7th, 1657

Laden with spoil of the South, fulfilled with the
      glory of achievement,
  And freshly crowned with never-dying fame,
Sweeping by shores where the names are the names of
      the victories of England,
  Across the Bay the squadron homeward came.

Proudly they came, but their pride was the pomp of a
      funeral at midnight,
  When dreader yet the lonely morrow looms;
Few are the words that are spoken, and faces are gaunt
      beneath the torchlight
  That does but darken more the nodding plumes.

Low on the field of his fame, past hope lay the Admiral
      triumphant,
  And fain to rest him after all his pain;
Yet for the love that he bore to his own land, ever
      unforgotten,
  He prayed to see the western hills again.

Fainter than stars in a sky long gray with the coming of
      the daybreak,
  Or sounds of night that fade when night is done,
So in the death-dawn faded the splendour and loud
      renown of warfare,
  And life of all its longings kept but one.

'Oh! to be there for an hour when the shade draws in
      beside the hedgerows,
  And falling apples wake the drowsy noon:
Oh! for the hour when the elms grow sombre and
      human in the twilight,
  And gardens dream beneath the rising moon.

'Only to look once more on the land of the memories
        of childhood,
    Forgetting weary winds and barren foam:
Only to bid farewell to the combe and the orchard and
        the moorland,
    And sleep at last among the fields of home!'

So he was silently praying, till now, when his strength
        was ebbing faster,
    The Lizard lay before them faintly blue;
Now on the gleaming horizon the white cliffs laughed
        along the coast-line,
    And now the forelands took the shapes they knew.

There lay the Sound and the Island with green leaves
        down beside the water,
    The town, the Hoe, the masts with sunset fired—
Dreams! ay, dreams of the dead! for the great heart
        faltered on the threshold,
    And darkness took the land his soul desired.

Gillespie

Riding at dawn, riding alone,
    Gillespie left the town behind;
Before he turned by the Westward road
    A horseman crossed him, staggering blind.

'The Devil's abroad in false Vellore,
    The Devil that stabs by night,' he said,
'Women and children, rank and file,
    Dying and dead, dying and dead.'

Without a word, without a groan,
　　Sudden and swift Gillespie turned,
The blood roared in his ears like fire,
　　Like fire the road beneath him burned.

He thundered back to Arcot gate,
　　He thundered up through Arcot town,
Before he thought a second thought
　　In the barrack yard he lighted down.

'Trumpeter, sound for the Light Dragoons,
　　Sound to saddle and spur,' he said;
'He that is ready may ride with me,
　　And he that can may ride ahead.'

Fierce and fain, fierce and fain,
　　Behind him went the troopers grim,
They rode as ride the Light Dragoons,
　　But never a man could ride with him.

Their rowels ripped their horses' sides,
　　Their hearts were red with a deeper goad,
But ever alone before them all
　　Gillespie rode, Gillespie rode.

Alone he came to false Vellore,
　　The walls were lined, the gates were barred;
Alone he walked where the bullets bit,
　　And called above to the Sergeant's Guard.

'Sergeant, Sergeant, over the gate,
　　Where are your officers all?' he said;
Heavily came the Sergeant's voice,
　　'There are two living and forty dead.'

'A rope, a rope', Gillespie cried:
　　They bound their belts to serve his need;
There was not a rebel behind the wall
　　But laid his barrel and drew his bead.

There was not a rebel among them all
　　But pulled his trigger and cursed his aim,
For lightly swung and rightly swung
　　Over the gate Gillespie came.

He dressed the line, he led the charge,
　　They swept the wall like a stream in spate,
And roaring over the roar they heard
　　The galloper guns that burst the gate.

Fierce and fain, fierce and fain,
　　The troopers rode the reeking flight:
The very stones remember still
　　The end of them that stab by night.

They've kept the tale a hundred years,
　　They'll keep the tale a hundred more:
Riding at dawn, riding alone,
　　Gillespie came to false Vellore.

Seringapatam

'The sleep that Tippoo Sahib sleeps
　　Heeds not the cry of man;
The faith that Tippoo Sahib keeps
　　No judge on earth may scan;
He is the lord of whom ye hold
　　Spirit and sense and limb,
Fetter and chain are all ye gain
　　Who dared to plead with him.'

Baird was bonny and Baird was young,
　　His heart was strong as steel,
But life and death in the balance hung,
　　For his wounds were ill to heal.
'Of fifty chains the Sultan gave
　　We have filled but forty-nine:
We dare not fail of the perfect tale
　　For all Golconda's mine.'

That was the hour when Lucas first
　　Leapt to his long renown;
Like summer rains his anger burst,
　　And swept their scruples down.
'Tell ye the lord to whom ye crouch,
　　His fetters bite their fill:
To save your oath I'll wear them both,
　　And step the lighter still.'

The seasons came, the seasons passed,
　　They watched their fellows die;
But still their thought was forward cast,
　　Their courage still was high.
Through tortured days and fevered nights
　　Their limbs alone were weak,
And year by year they kept their cheer,
　　And spoke as freemen speak.

But once a year, on the fourth of June,
　　Their speech to silence died,
And the silence beat to a soundless tune
　　And sang with a wordless pride;
Till when the Indian stars were bright,
　　And bells at home would ring,
To the fetters' clank they rose and drank
　　'England! God save the King!'

The years came, and the years went,
    The wheel full-circle rolled;
The tyrant's neck must yet be bent,
    The price of blood be told:
The city yet must hear the roar
    Of Baird's avenging guns,
And see him stand with lifted hand
    By Tippoo Sahib's sons.

The lads were bonny, the lads were young,
    But he claimed a pitiless debt;
Life and death in the balance hung,
    They watched it swing and set.
They saw him search with sombre eyes,
    They knew the place he sought;
They saw him feel for the hilted steel,
    They bowed before his thought.

But he – he saw the prison there
    In the old quivering heat,
Where merry hearts had met despair
    And died without defeat;
Where feeble hands had raised the cup
    For feebler lips to drain,
And one had worn with smiling scorn
    His double load of pain.

'The sleep that Tippoo Sahib sleeps
    Hears not the voice of man;
The faith that Tippoo Sahib keeps
    No earthly judge may scan;
For all the wrong your father wrought
    Your father's sons are free;
Where Lucas lay no tongue shall say
    That Mercy bound not me.'

March 28th–30th, 1898

The Gay Gordons

DARGAI, OCTOBER 20th, 1897

Who's for the Gathering, who's for the Fair?
    (*Gay goes the Gordon to a fight*)
The bravest of the brave are at deadlock there,
    (*Highlanders! march! by the right!*)
There are bullets by the hundred buzzing in the air;
There are bonny lads lying on the hillside bare;
But the Gordons know what the Gordons dare
    When they hear the pipers playing!

The happiest English heart to-day
    (*Gay goes the Gordon to a fight*)
Is the heart of the Colonel, hide it as he may
    (*Steady there! steady on the right!*)
He sees his work and he sees the way,
He knows his time and the word to say
And he's thinking of the tune that the Gordons play
    When he sets the pipers playing!

Rising, roaring, rushing like the tide,
    (*Gay goes the Gordon to a fight*)
They're up through the fire-zone, not to be denied;
    (*Bayonets! and charge! by the right!*)
Thirty bullets straight where the rest went wide,
And thirty lads are lying on the bare hillside;
But they passed in the hour of the Gordons' pride,
    To the skirl of the pipers' playing.

He Fell among Thieves

'Ye have robbed', said he, 'ye have slaughtered and made an end,
    Take your ill-got plunder, and bury the dead:
What will ye more of your guest and sometime friend?'
    'Blood for our blood', they said.

He laughed: 'If one may settle the score for five,
    I am ready; but let the reckoning stand till day:
I have loved the sunlight as dearly as any alive.'
    'You shall die at dawn', said they.

He flung his empty revolver down the slope,
    He climbed alone to the Eastward edge of the trees;
All night long in a dream untroubled of hope
    He brooded, clasping his knees.

He did not hear the monotonous roar that fills
    The ravine where the Yassin river sullenly flows;
He did not see the starlight on the Laspur hills,
    Or the far Afghan snows.

He saw the April noon on his books aglow,
    The wistaria trailing in at the window wide;
He heard his father's voice from the terrace below
    Calling him down to ride.

He saw the gray little church across the park,
    The mounds that hide the loved and honoured dead;
The Norman arch, the chancel softly dark,
    The brasses black and red.

He saw the School Close, sunny and green,
    The runner beside him, the stand by the parapet wall,
The distant tape, and the crowd roaring between
    His own name over all.

61

He saw the dark wainscot and timbered roof,
　　The long tables, and the faces merry and keen;
The College Eight and their trainer dining aloof,
　　The Dons on the daïs serene.

He watched the liner's stem ploughing the foam,
　　He felt her trembling speed and the thrash of her screw;
He heard her passengers' voices talking of home,
　　He saw the flag she flew.

And now it was dawn. He rose strong on his feet,
　　And strode to his ruined camp below the wood;
He drank the breath of the morning cool and sweet;
　　His murderers round him stood.

Light on the Laspur hills was broadening fast,
　　The blood-red snow-peaks chilled to a dazzling white:
He turned, and saw the golden circle at last,
　　Cut by the Eastern height.

'O glorious Life, Who dwellest in earth and sun,
　　I have lived, I praise and adore Thee.'
　　　　　　　　　　　　　　　A sword swept.
Over the pass the voices one by one
　　Faded, and the hill slept.

September, 1897

The Non-Combatant

Among a race high-handed, strong of heart,
Sea-rovers, conquerors, builders in the waste,
He had his birth; a nature too complete,
Eager and doubtful, no man's soldier sworn
And no man's chosen captain; born to fail,
A name without an echo: yet he too
Within the cloister of his narrow days
Fulfilled the ancestral rites, and kept alive
The eternal fire; it may be, not in vain;
For out of those who dropped a downward glance
Upon the weakling huddled at his prayers,
Perchance some looked beyond him, and then first
Beheld the glory, and what shrine it filled,
And to what Spirit sacred: or perchance
Some heard him chanting, though but to himself,
The old heroic names: and went their way:
And hummed his music on the march to death.

October, 1897

Clifton Chapel

This is the Chapel: here, my son,
    Your father thought the thoughts of youth,
And heard the words that one by one
    The touch of Life has turned to truth.
Here in a day that is not far
    You too may speak with noble ghosts
Of manhood and the vows of war
    You made before the Lord of Hosts.

To set the cause above renown,
  To love the game beyond the prize,
To honour, while you strike him down,
  The foe that comes with fearless eyes;
To count the life of battle good,
  And dear the land that gave you birth,
And dearer yet the brotherhood
  That binds the brave of all the earth –

My son, the oath is yours: the end
  Is His, Who built the world of strife,
Who gave His children Pain for friend,
  And Death for surest hope of life.
To-day and here the fight's begun,
  Of the great fellowship you're free;
Henceforth the School and you are one,
  And what You are, the race shall be.

God send you fortune: yet be sure,
  Among the lights that gleam and pass,
You'll live to follow none more pure
  Than that which glows on yonder brass:
'*Qui procul hinc*', the legend's writ, –
  The frontier-grave is far away –
'*Qui ante diem periit*:
  Sed miles, sed pro patria.'

Fidele's Grassy Tomb

The Squire sat propped in a pillowed chair,
His eyes were alive and clear of care,
But well he knew that the hour was come
To bid good-bye to his ancient home.

He looked on garden, wood, and hill,
He looked on the lake, sunny and still:
The last of earth that his eyes could see
Was the island church of Orchardleigh.

The last that his heart could understand
Was the touch of the tongue that licked his hand:
'Bury the dog at my feet', he said,
And his voice dropped, and the Squire was dead.

Now the dog was a hound of the Danish breed,
Staunch to love and strong at need:
He had dragged his master safe to shore
When the tide was ebbing at Elsinore.

From that day forth, as reason would,
He was named 'Fidele', and made it good:
When the last of the mourners left the door
Fidele was dead on the chantry floor.

They buried him there at his master's feet,
And all that heard of it deemed it meet:
The story went the round for years,
Till it came at last to the Bishop's ears.

Bishop of Bath and Wells was he,
Lord of the lords of Orchardleigh;
And he wrote to the Parson the strongest screed
That Bishop may write or Parson read.

The sum of it was that a soulless hound
Was known to be buried in hallowed ground:
From scandal sore the Church to save
They must take the dog from his master's grave.

The heir was far in a foreign land,
The Parson was wax to my Lord's command:
He sent for the Sexton and bade him make
A lonely grave by the shore of the lake.

The Sexton sat by the water's brink
Where he used to sit when he used to think:
He reasoned slow, but he reasoned it out,
And his argument left him free from doubt.

'A Bishop', he said, 'is the top of his trade;
But there's others can give him a start with the spade:
Yon dog, he carried the Squire ashore,
And a Christian couldn't ha' done no more.'

The grave was dug; the mason came
And carved on stone Fidele's name;
But the dog that the Sexton laid inside
Was a dog that never had lived or died.

So the Parson was praised, and the scandal stayed,
Till, a long time after, the church decayed,
And, laying the floor anew, they found
In the tomb of the Squire the bones of a hound.

As for the Bishop of Bath and Wells
No more of him the story tells;
Doubtless he lived as a Prelate and Prince,
And died and was buried a century since.

And whether his view was right or wrong
Has little to do with this my song;
Something we owe him, you must allow;
And perhaps he has changed his mind by now.

The Squire in the family chantry sleeps,
The marble still his memory keeps:
Remember, when the name you spell,
There rest Fidele's bones as well.

For the Sexton's grave you need not search,
'Tis a nameless mound by the island church:
An ignorant fellow, of humble lot –
But he knew one thing that a Bishop did not.

January 1st–4th, 1898

Gavotte

(OLD FRENCH)

Memories long in music sleeping,
  No more sleeping,
    No more dumb;
Delicate phantoms softly creeping
  Softly back from the old-world come.

Faintest odours around them straying,
  Suddenly straying
    In chambers dim;
Whispering silks in order swaying,
  Glimmering gems on shoulders slim:

Courage advancing strong and tender,
  Grace untender
    Fanning desire;
Suppliant conquest, proud surrender,
  Courtesy cold of hearts on fire –

Willowy billowy now they're bending,
   Low they're bending
     Down-dropt eyes;
Stately measure and stately ending,
   Music sobbing, and a dream that dies.

Nel Mezzo del Cammìn

Whisper it not that late in years
Sorrow shall fade and the world be brighter,
Life be freed of tremor and tears,
Heads be wiser and hearts be lighter.
Ah! but the dream that all endears,
The dream we sell for your pottage of truth –
Give us again the passion of youth,
Sorrow shall fade and the world be brighter.

April 2nd–4th, 1896

Imogen

A LADY OF TENDER AGE

Ladies, where were your bright eyes glancing,
   Where were they glancing yesternight?
Saw ye Imogen dancing, dancing,
   Imogen dancing all in white?
   Laughed she not with a pure delight,
   Laughed she not with a joy serene,
Stepped she not with a grace entrancing,
   Slenderly girt·in silken sheen?

All through the night from dusk to daytime
  Under her feet the hours were swift,
Under her feet the hours of playtime
  Rose and fell with a rhythmic lift:
  Music set her adrift, adrift,
  Music eddying towards the day
Swept her along as brooks in Maytime
  Carry the freshly falling May.

Ladies, life is a changing measure,
  Youth is a lilt that endeth soon;
Pluck ye never so fast at pleasure,
  Twilight follows the longest noon.
  Nay, but here is a lasting boon,
  Life for hearts that are old and chill,
Youth undying for hearts that treasure
  Imogen dancing, dancing still.

November 16th, 1896

Felix Antonius

(AFTER MARTIAL)

To-day, my friend is seventy-five;
  He tells his tale with no regret;
  His brave old eyes are steadfast yet,
His heart the lightest heart alive.

He sees behind him green and wide
  The pathway of his pilgrim years;
  He sees the shore, and dreadless hears
The whisper of the creeping tide.

69

For out of all his days, not one
    Has passed and left its unlaid ghost
    To seek a light for ever lost,
Or wail a deed for ever done.

So for reward of life-long truth
    He lives again, as good men can,
    Redoubling his allotted span
With memories of a stainless youth.

September 5th, 1895

The Invasion

Spring, they say, with his greenery
    Northward marches at last,
      Mustering thorn and elm;
Breezes rumour him conquering,
    Tell how Victory sits
      High on his glancing helm.

Smit with sting of his archery,
    Hardest ashes and oaks
      Burn at the root below:
Primrose, violet, daffodil,
    Start like blood where the shafts
      Light from his golden bow.

Here where winter oppresses us
    Still we listen and doubt,
      Dreading a hope betrayed:
Sore we long to be greeting him,
    Still we linger and doubt
      'What if his march be stayed?'

Folk in thrall to the enemy,
  Vanquished, tilling a soil
    Hateful and hostile grown;
Always wearily, warily,
  Feeding deep in the heart
    Passion they dare not own –

So we wait the deliverer;
  Surely soon shall he come,
    Soon shall his hour be due:
Spring shall come with his greenery,
  Life be lovely again,
    Earth be the home we knew.

November 28th–29th, 1897

Ireland, Ireland

Down thy valleys, Ireland, Ireland,
  Down thy valleys green and sad,
Still thy spirit wanders wailing,
  Wanders wailing, wanders mad.

Long ago that anguish took thee,
  Ireland, Ireland, green and fair,
Spoilers strong in darkness took thee,
  Broke thy heart and left thee there.

Down thy valleys, Ireland, Ireland,
  Still thy spirit wanders mad;
All too late they love that wronged thee,
  Ireland, Ireland, green and sad.

March, 1898

Moonset

Past seven o'clock: time to be gone;
Twelfth-night's over and dawn shivering up:
A hasty cut of the loaf, a steaming cup,
Down to the door, and there is Coachman John.

Ruddy of cheek is John and bright of eye;
But John it appears has none of your grins and winks;
Civil enough, but short: perhaps he thinks:
Words come once in a mile, and always dry.

Has he a mind or not? I wonder; but soon
We turn through a leafless wood, and there to the right,
Like a sun bewitched in alien realms of night,
Mellow and yellow and rounded hangs the moon.

Strangely near she seems, and terribly great:
The world is dead: why are we travelling still?
Nightmare silence grips my struggling will;
We are driving for ever and ever to find a gate.

'When you come to consider the moon', says John at last,
And stops, to feel his footing and take his stand;
'And then there's some will say there's never a hand
That made the world!'
                        A flick, and the gates are passed.

Out of the dim magical moonlit park,
Out to the workday road and wider skies:
There's a warm flush in the East where day's to rise,
And I'm feeling the better for Coachman John's remark.

June 7th, 1898

Hymn

O Lord Almighty, Thou whose hands
   Despair and victory give;
In whom, though tyrants tread their lands,
   The souls of nations live;

Thou wilt not turn Thy face away
   From those who work Thy will,
But send Thy peace on hearts that pray,
   And guard Thy people still.

Remember not the days of shame,
   The hands with rapine dyed,
The wavering will, the baser aim,
   The brute material pride:

Remember, Lord, the years of faith,
   The spirits humbly brave,
The strength that died defying death,
   The love that loved the slave:

The race that strove to rule Thine earth
   With equal laws unbought:
Who bore for Truth the pangs of birth,
   And brake the bonds of Thought.

Remember how, since time began,
   Thy dark eternal mind
Through lives of men that fear not man
   Is light for all mankind.

Thou wilt not turn Thy face away
   From those who work Thy will,
But send Thy strength on hearts that pray
   For strength to serve Thee still.

January 30th–31st, 1898

The Sailing of the Long-Ships

OCTOBER, 1899

They saw the cables loosened, they saw the gangways cleared,
They heard the women weeping, they heard the men that cheered;
Far off, far off, the tumult faded and died away,
And all alone the sea-wind came singing up the Bay.

'I came by Cape St Vincent, I came by Trafalgar,
I swept from Torres Vedras to golden Vigo Bar,
I saw the beacons blazing that fired the world with light
When down their ancient highway your fathers passed to fight.

'O race of tireless fighters, flushed with a youth renewed,
Right well the wars of Freedom befit the Sea-kings' brood;
Yet as ye go forget not the fame of yonder shore,
The fame ye owe your fathers and the old time before.

'Long-suffering were the Sea-kings, they were not swift to kill,
But when the sands had fallen they waited no man's will;
Though all the world forbade them, they counted not nor cared,
They weighed not help or hindrance, they did the thing they dared.

'The Sea-kings loved not boasting, they cursed not him that cursed,
They honoured all men duly, and him that faced them, first;
They strove and knew not hatred, they smote and toiled to save,
They tended whom they vanquished, they praised the fallen brave.

'Their fame's on Torres Vedras, their fame's on Vigo Bar,
Far-flashed to Cape St Vincent it burns from Trafalgar;
Mark as ye go the beacons that woke the world with light
When down their ancient highway your fathers passed to fight.'

October 17th, 1899

Waggon Hill

Drake in the North Sea grimly prowling,
    Treading his dear *Revenge's* deck,
Watched, with the sea-dogs round him growling,
    Galleons drifting wreck by wreck.
    'Fetter and Faith for England's neck,
  Faggot and Father, Saint and chain, –
Yonder the Devil and all go howling,
    Devon, O Devon, in wind and rain!'

Drake at the last off Nombre lying,
    Knowing the night that toward him crept,
Gave to the sea-dogs round him crying
    This for a sign before he slept: –
    'Pride of the West! What Devon hath kept
  Devon shall keep on tide or main;
Call to the storm, and drive them flying,
    Devon, O Devon, in wind and rain!'

Valour of England gaunt and whitening,
    Far in a South land brought to bay,
Locked in a death-grip all day tightening,
    Waited the end in twilight gray.
    Battle and storm and the sea-dog's way!
  Drake from his long rest turned again,
Victory lit thy steel with lightning,
    Devon, O Devon, in wind and rain!

April 16th, 1900

The Volunteer

'He leapt to arms unbidden,
    Unneeded, over-bold;
His face by earth is hidden,
    His heart in earth is cold.

'Curse on the reckless daring
    That could not wait the call,
The proud fantastic bearing
    That would be first to fall!'

O tears of human passion,
    Blur not the image true;
This was not folly's fashion,
    This was the man we knew.

December 5th, 1899

The Only Son

O bitter wind toward the sunset blowing,
    What of the dales to-night?
In yonder gray old hall what fires are glowing,
    What ring of festal light?

'*In the great window as the day was dwindling
    I saw an old man stand;
His head was proudly held and his eyes kindling,
    But the list shook in his hand.*'

O wind of twilight, was there no word uttered,
    No sound of joy or wail?
'*"A great fight and a good death", he muttered;
    "Trust him, he would not fail."*'

What of the chamber dark where she was lying
  For whom all life is done?
'*Within her heart she rocks a dead child, crying*
  "*My son, my little son.*"'

January 15th, 1900

The Grenadier's Good-Bye

When Lieutenant Murray fell, the only words he
spoke were 'Forward, Grenadiers!' Press Telegram

Here they halted, here once more
  Hand from hand was rent;
Here his voice above the roar
  Rang, and on they went.
Yonder out of sight they crossed,
  Yonder died the cheers;
One word lives where all is lost –
  'Forward, Grenadiers!'

This alone he asked of fame,
  This alone of pride;
Still with this he faced the flame,
  Answered Death, and died.
Crest of battle sunward tossed,
  Song of the marching years,
This shall live though all be lost –
  'Forward, Grenadiers!'

March 28th, 1902

The Schoolfellow

Our game was his but yesteryear;
   We wished him back; we could not know
The self-same hour we missed him here
   He led the line that broke the foe.

Blood-red behind our guarded posts
   Sank as of old the dying day;
The battle ceased; the mingled hosts
   Weary and cheery went their way:

'Tomorrow well may bring', we said,
   'As fair a fight, as clear a sun.'
Dear lad, before the word was sped,
   For evermore thy goal was won.

November 10th, 1899

On Spion Kop

Foremost of all on battle's fiery steep
Here VERTUE fell, and here he sleeps his sleep.
A fairer name no Roman ever gave
To stand sole monument on Valour's grave.

The School at War

All night before the brink of death
   In fitful sleep the army lay,
For through the dream that stilled their breath
   Too gauntly glared the coming day.

But we, within whose blood there leaps
   The fulness of a life as wide
As Avon's water where he sweeps
   Seaward at last with Severn's tide,

We heard beyond the desert night
   The murmur of the fields we knew,
And our swift souls with one delight
   Like homing swallows Northward flew.

We played again the immortal games,
   And grappled with the fierce old friends,
And cheered the dead undying names,
   And sang the song that never ends;

Till, when the hard, familiar bell
   Told that the summer night was late,
Where long ago we said farewell,
   We said farewell by the old gate.

'O Captains unforgot', they cried,
   'Come you again or come no more,
Across the world you keep the pride,
   Across the world we mark the score.'

May 21st, 1901

By the Hearth-Stone

By the hearth-stone
She sits alone,
   The long night bearing:
With eyes that gleam
Into the dream
   Of the firelight staring.

Low and more low
The dying glow
   Burns in the embers;
She nothing heeds
And nothing needs –
   Only remembers.

May 16th, 1899

Peace

No more to watch by Night's eternal shore,
   With England's chivalry at dawn to ride;
No more defeat, faith, victory – O! no more
   A cause on earth for which we might have died.

June 21st, 1902

Commemoration

I sat by the granite pillar, and sunlight fell
  Where the sunlight fell of old,
And the hour was the hour my heart remembered well,
  And the sermon rolled and rolled
As it used to roll when the place was still unhaunted,
  And the strangest tale in the world was still untold.

And I knew that of all this rushing of urgent sound
  That I so clearly heard,
The green young forest of saplings clustered round
  Was heeding not one word:
Their heads were bowed in a still serried patience
  Such as an angel's breath could never have stirred.

For some were already away to the hazardous pitch,
  Or lining the parapet wall,
And some were in glorious battle, or great and rich,
  Or throned in a college hall:
And among the rest was one like my own young phantom,
  Dreaming for ever beyond my utmost call.

'O Youth,' the preacher was crying, 'deem not thou
  Thy life is thine alone;
Thou bearest the will of the ages, seeing how
  They built thee bone by bone,
And within thy blood the Great Age sleeps sepulchred
  Till thou and thine shall roll away the stone.

'Therefore the days are coming when thou shalt burn
  With passion whitely hot;
Rest shall be rest no more; thy feet shall spurn
  All that thy hand hath got;
And One that is stronger shall gird thee, and lead thee swiftly
  Whither, O heart of Youth, thou wouldest not.'

And the School passed; and I saw the living and dead
    Set in their seats again,
And I longed to hear them speak of the word that was said,
    But I knew that I longed in vain.
And they stretched forth their hands, and the wind of
      the spirit took them
    Lightly as drifted leaves on an endless plain.

July 7th, 1901

Sráhmandázi

Deep embowered beside the forest river,
    Where the flame of sunset only falls,
Lapped in silence lies the House of Dying,
    House of them to whom the twilight calls.

There within when day was near to ending,
    By her lord a woman young and strong,
By his chief a songman old and stricken
    Watched together till the hour of song.

'O my songman, now the bow is broken,
    Now the arrows one by one are sped,
Sing to me the song of Sráhmandázi,
    Sráhmandázi, home of all the dead.'

Then the songman, flinging wide his songnet,
    On the last token laid his master's hand,
While he sang the song of Sráhmandázi,
    None but dying men can understand.

'Yonder sun that fierce and fiery-hearted
    Marches down the sky to vanish soon,
At the self-same hour in Sráhmandázi
    Rises pallid like the rainy moon.

'There he sees the heroes by their river,
    Where the great fish daily upward swim;
Yet they are but shadows hunting shadows,
    Phantom fish in waters drear and dim.

'There he sees the kings among their headmen,
    Women weaving, children playing games;
Yet they are but shadows ruling shadows,
    Phantom folk with dim forgotten names.

'Bid farewell to all that most thou lovest,
    Tell thy heart thy living life is done;
All the days and deeds of Sráhmandázi
    Are not worth an hour of yonder sun.'

Dreamily the chief from out the songnet
    Drew his hand and touched the woman's head:
'Know they not, then, love in Sráhmandázi?
    Has a king no bride among the dead?'

Then the songman answered, 'O my master,
    Love they know, but none may learn it there;
Only souls that reach that land together
    Keep their troth and find the twilight fair.

'Thou art still a king, and at thy passing
    By thy latest word must all abide:
If thou willest, here am I, thy songman;
    If thou lovest, here is she, thy bride.'

Hushed and dreamy lay the House of Dying,
    Dreamily the sunlight upward failed,
Dreamily the chief on eyes that loved him
    Looked with eyes the coming twilight veiled.

Then he cried, 'My songman, I am passing;
    Let her live, her life is but begun;
All the days and nights of Sráhmandázi
    Are not worth an hour of yonder sun.'

Yet, when there within the House of Dying
　　The last silence held the sunset air,
Not alone he came to Sráhmandázi,
　　Not alone she found the twilight fair:

While the songman, far beneath the forest
　　Sang of Sráhmandázi all night through,
'Lovely be thy name, O Land of shadows,
　　Land of meeting, Land of all the true!'

April, 1902

Outward Bound

Dear Earth, near Earth, the clay that made us men,
　　The land we sowed,
　　The hearth that glowed –
　　　O Mother, must we bid farewell to thee?
Fast dawns the last dawn, and what shall comfort then
　　The lonely hearts that roam the outer sea?

Gray wakes the daybreak, the shivering sails are set,
　　To misty deeps
　　The channel sweeps –
　　　O Mother, think on us who think on thee!
Earth-home, birth-home, with love remember yet
　　The sons in exile on the eternal sea.

January 30th, 1899

O Pulchritudo

O Saint whose thousand shrines our feet have trod
  And our eyes loved thy lamp's eternal beam,
Dim earthly radiance of the Unknown God,
  Hope of the darkness, light of them that dream,
Far off, far off and faint, O glimmer on
Till we thy pilgrims from the road are gone.

O Word whose meaning every sense hath sought,
  Voice of the teeming field and grassy mound,
Deep-whispering fountain of the wells of thought,
  Will of the wind and soul of all sweet sound,
Far off, far off and faint, O murmur on
Till we thy pilgrims from the road are gone.

May 19th, 1902

In July

His beauty bore no token,
    No sign our gladness shook;
With tender strength unbroken
    The hand of Life he took:
But the summer flowers were falling,
    Falling and fading away,
And mother birds were calling,
      Crying and calling
    For their loves that would not stay.

He knew not Autumn's chillness,
    Nor Winter's wind nor Spring's;
He lived with Summer's stillness
    And sun and sunlit things:
But when the dusk was falling
    He went the shadowy way,
And one more heart is calling,
        Crying and calling
    For the love that would not stay.

November 1st, 1898

From Generation to Generation

O son of mine, when dusk shall find thee bending
    Between a gravestone and a cradle's head –
Between the love whose name is loss unending
    And the young love whose thoughts are liker dread, –
Thou too shalt groan at heart that all thy spending
    Cannot repay the dead, the hungry dead.

March 26th, 1902

When I Remember

When I remember that the day will come
    For this our love to quit his land of birth,
    And bid farewell to all the ways of earth
With lips that must for evermore be dumb,

Then creep I silent from the stirring hum,
   And shut away the music and the mirth,
   And reckon up what may be left of worth
When hearts are cold and love's own body numb.

Something there must be that I know not here,
Or know too dimly through the symbol dear;
   Some touch, some beauty, only guessed by this –
If He that made us loves, it shall replace,
Beloved, even the vision of thy face
   And deep communion of thine inmost kiss.

September 29th, 1899

Rondel

Though I wander far-off ways,
   Dearest, never doubt thou me:

Mine is not the love that strays,
Though I wander far-off ways:

Faithfully for all my days
   I have vowed myself to thee:
Though I wander far-off ways,
   Dearest, never doubt thou me.

December 4th, 1899

Rondel

Long ago to thee I gave
Body, soul, and all I have –
   Nothing in the world I keep:

All that in return I crave
Is that thou accept the slave
Long ago to thee I gave –
Body, soul, and all I have.

Had I more to share or save,
I would give as give the brave,
   Stooping not to part the heap;
Long ago to thee I gave
Body, soul, and all I have –
   Nothing in the world I keep.

Balade

I cannot tell, of twain beneath this bond,
Which one in grief the other goes beyond, –
Narcissus, who to end the pain he bore
Died of the love that could not help him more;
Or I, that pine because I cannot see
The lady who is queen and love to me.

Nay – for Narcissus, in the forest pond
Seeing his image, made entreaty fond,
'Beloved, comfort on my longing pour';
So for a while he soothed his passion sore;
So cannot I, for all too far is she –
The lady who is queen and love to me.

But since that I have Love's true colours donned,
I in his service will not now despond,
For in extremes Love yet can all restore:
So till her beauty walks the world no more
All day remembered in my hope shall be
The lady who is queen and love to me.

November 28th, 1900

The Viking's Song

When I thy lover first
   Shook out my canvas free
And like a pirate burst
   Into that dreaming sea,
The land knew no such thirst
   As then tormented me.

Now when at eve returned
   I near that shore divine,
Where once but watch-fires burned
   I see thy beacon shine,
And know the land hath learned
   Desire that welcomes mine.

1900

Yattendon

Among the woods and tillage
  That fringe the topmost downs,
All lonely lies the village,
  Far off from seas and towns.
Yet when her own folk slumbered
  I heard within her street
Murmur of men unnumbered
  And march of myriad feet.

For all she lies so lonely,
  Far off from towns and seas,
The village holds not only
  The roofs beneath her trees:
While Life is sweet and tragic
  And Death is veiled and dumb,
Hither, by singer's magic,
  The pilgrim world must come.

July 14th, 1899

Among the Tombs

She is a lady fair and wise,
  Her heart her counsel keeps,
And well she knows of time that flies
  And tide that onward sweeps;
But still she sits with restless eyes
  Where Memory sleeps —
  Where Memory sleeps.

Ye that have heard the whispering dead
    In every wind that creeps,
Or felt the stir that strains the lead
    Beneath the mounded heaps,
Tread softly, ah! more softly tread
    Where Memory sleeps –
    Where Memory sleeps.

January 25th, 1899

A Sower

With sanguine looks
    And rolling walk
Among the rooks
    He loved to stalk,

While on the land
    With gusty laugh
From a full hand
    He scattered chaff.

Now that within
    His spirit sleeps
A harvest thin
    The sickle reaps;

But the dumb fields
    Desire his tread,
And no earth yields
    A wheat more red.

March 30th, 1902

The Best School of All

It's good to see the School we knew,
　　The land of youth and dream,
To greet again the rule we knew
　　Before we took the stream:
Though long we've missed the sight of her,
　　Our hearts may not forget;
We've lost the old delight of her,
　　We keep her honour yet.

We'll honour yet the School we knew,
　　The best School of all:
We'll honour yet the rule we knew,
　　Till the last bell call.
For, working days or holidays,
And glad or melancholy days,
They were great days and jolly days
　　At the best School of all.

The stars and sounding vanities
　　That half the crowd bewitch,
What are they but inanities
　　To him that treads the pitch?
And where's the wealth, I'm wondering,
　　Could buy the cheers that roll
When the last charge goes thundering
　　Beneath the twilight goal?

The men that tanned the hide of us,
　　Our daily foes and friends,
They shall not lose their pride of us
　　Howe'er the journey ends.
Their voice, to us who sing of it,
　　No more its message bears,
But the round world shall ring of it
　　And all we are be theirs.

To speak of Fame a venture is,
    There's little here can bide,
But we may face the centuries,
    And dare the deepening tide:
For though the dust that's part of us
    To dust again be gone,
Yet here shall beat the heart of us –
    The School we handed on!

We'll honour yet the School we knew,
    The best School of all:
We'll honour yet the rule we knew,
    Till the last bell call.
For, working days or holidays,
And glad or melancholy days,
They were great days and jolly days
    At the best School of all.

March 19th, 1899

The Bright Medusa

1807

She's the daughter of the breeze,
She's the darling of the seas,
    And we call her, if you please, the bright *Medu – sa*;
From beneath her bosom bare
To the snakes among her hair
    She's a flash o' golden light, the bright *Medu – sa*.

When the ensign dips above
And the guns are all for love,
    She's as gentle as a dove, the bright *Medu – sa*;
But when the shot's in rack
And her forestay flies the Jack,
    He's a merry man would slight the bright *Medu – sa*.

When she got the word to go
Up to Monte Video,
    There she found the river low, the bright *Medu – sa;*
So she tumbled out her guns
And a hundred of her sons,
    And she taught the Dons to fight the bright *Medu – sa.*

When the foeman can be found
With the pluck to cross her ground,
    First she walks him round and round, the bright *Medu – sa;*
Then she rakes him fore and aft
Till he's just a jolly raft,
    And she grabs him like a kite, the bright *Medu – sa.*

She's the daughter of the breeze,
She's the darling of the seas,
    And you'll call her, if you please, the bright *Medu – sa;*
For till England's sun be set –
And it's not for setting yet –
    She shall bear her name by right, the bright *Medu – sa.*

Northumberland

'THE OLD AND BOLD'

When England sets her banner forth
    And bids her armour shine,
She'll not forget the famous North,
    The lads of moor and Tyne;
And when the loving-cup's in hand
    And Honour leads the cry,
They know not old Northumberland
    Who'll pass her memory by.

When Nelson sailed for Trafalgar
    With all his country's best,
He held them dear as brothers are,
    But one beyond the rest.

For when the fleet with heroes manned
　　To clear the decks began,
The boast of old Northumberland
　　He sent to lead the van.

Himself by *Victory*'s bulwarks stood
　　And cheered to see the sight;
'That noble fellow Collingwood,
　　How bold he goes to fight!'
Love, that the league of Ocean spanned,
　　Heard him as face to face;
'What would he give, Northumberland,
　　To share our pride of place?'

The flag that goes the world around
　　And flaps on every breeze
Has never gladdened fairer ground
　　Or kinder hearts than these.
So when the loving-cup's in hand
　　And Honour leads the cry,
They know not old Northumberland
　　Who'll pass her memory by.

April 19th–20th, 1900

The Old Superb

The wind was rising easterly, the morning sky was blue,
　　The Straits before us opened wide and free;
We looked towards the Admiral, where high the Peter flew,
　　And all our hearts were dancing like the sea.
'The French are gone to Martinique with four-and-twenty sail!
　　The Old *Superb* is old and foul and slow,
But the French are gone to Martinique, and Nelson's on the trail,
　　And where he goes the Old *Superb* must go!'

So Westward ho! for Trinidad and Eastward ho! for Spain,
  And 'Ship ahoy!' a hundred times a day;
Round the world if need be, and round the world again,
  With a lame duck lagging all the way!

The Old *Superb* was barnacled and green as grass below,
  Her sticks were only fit for stirring grog;
The pride of all her midshipmen was silent long ago,
  And long ago they ceased to heave the log.
Four year out from home she was, and ne'er a week in port,
  And nothing save the guns aboard her bright;
But Captain Keats he knew the game, and swore to share the sport,
  For he never yet came in too late to fight.

So Westward ho! for Trinidad and Eastward ho! for Spain,
  And 'Ship ahoy!' a hundred times a day;
Round the world if need be, and round the world again,
  With a lame duck lagging all the way!

'Now up, my lads!' the Captain cried, 'for sure the case were hard
  If longest out were first to fall behind.
Aloft, aloft with studding sails, and lash them on the yard,
  For night and day the Trades are driving blind!'
So all day long and all day long behind the fleet we crept,
  And how we fretted none but Nelson guessed;
But every night the Old *Superb* she sailed when others slept,
  Till we ran the French to earth with all the rest!

Oh, 'twas Westward ho! for Trinidad and Eastward ho! for Spain,
  And 'Ship ahoy!' a hundred times a day;
Round the world if need be, and round the world again,
  With a lame duck lagging all the way!

February 3rd, 1904

96

Homeward Bound

After long labouring in the windy ways,
  On smooth and shining tides
  Swiftly the great ship glides,
    Her storms forgot, her weary watches past;
Northward she glides, and through the enchanted haze
    Faint on the verge her far hope dawns at last.

The phantom sky-line of a shadowy down,
  Whose pale white cliffs below
  Through sunny mist aglow
    Like noon-day ghosts of summer moonshine gleam –
Soft as old sorrow, bright as old renown,
    There lies the home of all our mortal dream.

April on Waggon Hill

Lad, and can you rest now,
  There beneath your hill?
Your hands are on your breast now,
  But is your heart so still?
'Twas the right death to die, lad,
  A gift without regret,
But unless truth's a lie, lad,
  You dream of Devon yet.

Ay, ay, the year's awaking,
  The fire's among the ling,
The beechen hedge is breaking,
  The curlew's on the wing;
Primroses are out, lad,
  On the high banks of Lee,
And the sun stirs the trout, lad,
  From Brendon to the sea.

97

I know what's in your heart, lad, –
    The mare he used to hunt –
And her blue market-cart, lad,
    With posies tied in front –
We miss them from the moor road,
    They're getting old to roam,
The road they're on's a sure road
    And nearer, lad, to home.

Your name, the name they cherish?
    'Twill fade, lad, 'tis true:
But stone and all may perish
    With little loss to you.
While fame's fame you're Devon, lad,
    The Glory of the West;
Till the roll's called in heaven, lad,
    You may well take your rest.

Epistle

To Colonel Francis Edward Younghusband

Across the Western World, the Arabian Sea,
The Hundred Kingdoms and the Rivers Three,
Beyond the rampart of Himálayan snows,
And up the road that only Rumour knows,
Unchecked, old friend, from Devon to Thibet,
Friendship and Memory dog your footsteps yet.

Let not the scornful ask me what avails
So small a pack to follow mighty trails:
Long since I saw what difference must be
Between a stream like you, a ditch like me.

This drains a garden and a homely field
Which scarce at times a living current yield;
The other from the high lands of his birth
Plunges through rocks and spurns the pastoral earth,
Then settling silent to his deeper course,
Draws in his fellows to augment his force,
Becomes a name, and broadening as he goes,
Gives power and purity wher'er he flows,
Till, great enough for any commerce grown,
He links all nations while he serves his own.

Soldier, explorer, statesman, what in truth
Have you in common with homekeeping youth?
'Youth' comes your answer like an echo faint;
And youth it was that made us first acquaint.
Do you remember when the Downs were white
With the March dust from highways glaring bright,
How you and I, like yachts that toss the foam,
From Penpole Fields came stride and stride for home?
One grimly leading, one intent to pass,
Mile after mile we measured road and grass,
Twin silent shadows, till the hour was done,
The shadows parted and the stouter won.
Since then I know one thing beyond appeal –
How runs from stem to stern a trimbuilt keel.
Another day – but that's not mine to tell,
The man in front does not observe so well;
Though, spite of all these five-and-twenty years,
As clear as life our schoolday scene appears.
The guarded course, the barriers and the rope;
The runners, stripped of all but shivering hope;
The starter's good gray head; the sudden hush;
The stern white line; the half-unconscious rush;
The deadly bend, the pivot of our fate;
The rope again; the long green level straight;
The lane of heads, the cheering half unheard;
The dying spurt, the tape, the judge's word.

You, too, I doubt not, from your Lama's hall
Can see the Stand above the worn old wall,
Where then they clamoured as our race we sped,
Where now they number our heroic dead.
As clear as life you, too, can hear the sound
Of voices once for all by 'lock-up' bound,
And see the flash of eyes still nobly bright
But in the 'Bigside scrimmage' lost to sight.

Old loves, old rivalries, old happy times,
These well may move your memory and my rhymes;
These are the Past; but there is that, my friend,
Between us two, that has nor time nor end.
Though wide apart the lines our fate has traced
Since those far shadows of our boyhood raced,
In the dim region all men must explore –
The mind's Thibet, where none has gone before –
Rounding some shoulder of the lonely trail
We met once more, and raised a lusty hail.

'Forward!' cried one, 'for us no beaten track,
No city continuing, no turning back:
The past we love not for its being past,
But for its hope and ardour forward cast:
The victories of our youth we count for gain
Only because they steeled our hearts to pain,
And hold no longer even Clifton great
Save as she schooled our wills to serve the State.
Nay, England's self, whose thousand-year-old name
Burns in our blood like ever-smouldering flame,
Whose Titan shoulders as the world are wide
And her great pulses like the Ocean tide,
Lives but to bear the hopes we shall not see –
Dear mortal Mother of the race to be.'

Thereto you answered, 'Forward! in God's name:
I own no lesser law, no narrower claim.

A freeman's Reason well might think it scorn
To toil for those who may be never born,
But for some Cause not wholly out of ken,
Some all-directing Will that works with men,
Some Universal under which may fall
The minor premiss of our effort small;
In Whose unending purpose, though we cease,
We find our impulse and our only peace.'

So passed our greeting, till we turned once more,
I to my desk and you to rule Indore.
To meet again – ah! when? Yet once we met,
And to one dawn our faces still are set.

Exeter
September 10th, 1904

Sacramentum Supremum

MUKDEN, MARCH 6th, 1905

Ye that with me have fought and failed and fought
    To the last desperate trench of battle's crest,
Not yet to sleep, not yet; our work is nought;
    On that last trench the fate of all may rest.
Draw near, my friends; and let your thoughts be high;
    Great hearts are glad when it is time to give;
Life is no life to him that dares not die,
    And death no death to him that dares to live.

Draw near together; none be last or first;
   We are no longer names, but one desire;
With the same burning of the soul we thirst,
   And the same wine to-night shall quench our fire.
Drink! to our fathers who begot us men,
   To the dead voices that are never dumb;
Then to the land of all our loves, and then
   To the long parting, and the age to come.

1905

The Hundredth Year

'Drake, and Blake, and Nelson's mighty name'

The stars were faint in heaven
   That saw the Old Year die;
The dream-white mist of Devon
   Shut in the seaward sky:
Before the dawn's unveiling
I heard three voices hailing,
I saw three ships come sailing
   With lanterns gleaming high.

The first he cried defiance –
   A full-mouthed voice and bold –
'On God be our reliance,
   Our hope the Spaniard's gold!
With a still, stern ambuscado,
With a roaring escalado,
We'll sack their Eldorado
   And storm their dungeon hold!'

Then slowly spake the second –
    A great sad voice and deep –
'When all your gold is reckoned,
    There is but this to keep:
To stay the foe from fooling,
To learn the heathen schooling,
To live and die sea-ruling,
    And home at last to sleep.'

But the third matched in beauty
    The dawn that flushed afar;
'O sons of England, Duty
    Is England's morning star:
Then Fame's eternal splendour
Be theirs who well defend her,
And theirs who fain would bend her
    The night of Trafalgar!'

December, 1904

The Mossrose

Walking to-day in your garden, O gracious lady,
Little you thought as you turned in that alley remote and shady,
And gave me a rose and asked if I knew its savour –
The old-world scent of the mossrose, flower of a bygone favour –

Little you thought as you waited the word of appraisement,
Laughing at first and then amazed at my amazement,
That the rose you gave was a gift already cherished,
And the garden whence you plucked it a garden long perished.

But I – I saw that garden, with its one treasure
The tiny mossrose, tiny even by childhood's measure,
And the long morning shadow of the dusty laurel,
And a boy and a girl beneath it, flushed with a childish quarrel.

She wept for her one little bud: but he, outreaching
The hand of brotherly right, would take it for all her beseeching:
And she flung her arms about him, and gave like a sister,
And laughed at her own tears, and wept again when he kissed her.

So the rose is mine long since, and whenever I find it
And drink again the sharp sweet scent of the moss behind it,
I remember the tears of a child, and her love and her laughter,
And the morning shadows of youth and the night that fell thereafter.

Ave, Soror

I left behind the ways of care,
  The crowded hurrying hours,
I breathed again the woodland air,
  I plucked the woodland flowers:

Bluebells as yet but half awake,
  Primroses pale and cool,
Anemones like stars that shake
  In a green twilight pool –

On these still lay the enchanted shade,
  The magic April sun;
With my own child a child I strayed
  And thought the years were one.

As through the copse she went and came
  My senses lost their truth;
I called her by the dear dead name
  That sweetened all my youth.

April 12th, 1906

Midway

Turn back, my Soul, no longer set
  Thy peace upon the years to come:
Turn back, the land of thy regret
  Holds nothing doubtful, nothing dumb.

There are the voices, there the scenes
  That make thy life in living truth
A tale of heroes and of queens,
  Fairer than all the hopes of youth.

December, 1907

Amore Altiero

Since thou and I have wandered from the highway
  And found with hearts reborn
This swift and unimaginable byway
  Unto the hills of morn,
Shall not our love disdain the unworthy uses
  Of the old time outworn?

I'll not entreat thy half-unwilling graces
   With humbly folded palms,
Nor seek to shake thy proud defended places
   With noise of vague alarms,
Nor ask against my fortune's grim pursuing
   The refuge of thy arms.

Thou'lt not withhold for pleasure vain and cruel
   That which has long been mine,
Nor overheap with briefly burning fuel
   A fire of flame divine,
Nor yield the key for life's profaner voices
   To brawl within the shrine.

But thou shalt tell me of thy queenly pleasure
   All that I must fulfil,
And I'll receive from out my royal treasure
   What golden gifts I will,
So that two realms supreme and undisputed
   Shall be one kingdom still.

And our high hearts shall praise the beauty hidden
   In starry-minded scorn
By the same Lord who hath His servants bidden
   To seek with eyes new-born
This swift and unimaginable byway
   Unto the hills of morn.

Love and Grief

One day, when Love and Summer both were young,
   Love in a garden found my lady weeping;
Whereat, when he to kiss her would have sprung,
   I stayed his childish leaping.

'Forbear', said I, 'she is not thine to-day;
  Subdue thyself in silence to await her;
If thou dare call her from Death's side away
  Thou art no Love, but traitor.'

Yet did he run, and she his kiss received,
  'She is twice mine', he cried, 'since she is troubled:
I knew but half, and now I see her grieved
  My part in her is doubled.'

Against Oblivion

Cities drowned in olden time
Keep, they say, a magic chime
Rolling up from far below
When the moon-led waters flow.

So within me, ocean deep,
Lies a sunken world asleep.
Lest its bells forget to ring,
Memory! set the tide a-swing!

Fond Counsel

O Youth, beside thy silver-springing fountain,
In sight and hearing of thy father's cot,
These and the morning woods, the lonely mountain,
These are thy peace, although thou know'st it not.
Wander not yet where noon's unpitying glare
Beats down the toilers in the city bare;
Forsake not yet, not yet, the homely plot,
O Youth, beside thy silver-springing fountain.

March 12th, 1908

The Wanderer

To Youth there comes a whisper out of the west:
　'O loiterer, hasten where there waits for thee
A life to build, a love therein to nest,
　And a man's work, serving the age to be.'

Peace, peace awhile! Before his tireless feet
　Hill beyond hill the road in sunlight goes;
He breathes the breath of morning, clear and sweet,
　And his eyes love the high eternal snows.

The Adventurers

Over the downs in sunlight clear
Forth we went in the spring of the year:
Plunder of April's gold we sought,
Little of April's anger thought.

Caught in a copse without defence
Low we crouched to the rain-squall dense:
Sure, if misery man can vex,
There it beat on our bended necks.

Yet when again we wander on
Suddenly all that gloom is gone:
Under and over through the wood,
Life is astir, and life is good.

Violets purple, violets white,
Delicate windflowers dancing light,
Primrose, mercury, moscatel,
Shimmer in diamonds round the dell.

Squirrel is climbing swift and lithe,
Chiff-chaff whetting his airy scythe,
Woodpecker whirrs his rattling rap,
Ringdove flies with a sudden clap.

Rook is summoning rook to build,
Dunnock his beak with moss has filled,
Robin is bowing in coat-tails brown,
Tomtit chattering upside down.

Well is it seen that every one
Laughs at the rain and loves the sun;
We too laughed with the wildwood crew,
Laughed till the sky once more was blue.

Homeward over the downs we went
Soaked to the heart with sweet content;
April's anger is swift to fall,
April's wonder is worth it all.

An Essay on Criticism

'Tis hard to say if greater waste of time
Is seen in writing or in reading rhyme;
But, of the two, less dangerous it appears
To tire our own than poison others' ears.
Time was, the owner of a peevish tongue,
The pebble of his wrath unheeding flung,
Saw the faint ripples touch the shore and cease,
And in the duckpond all again was peace.
But since that Science on our eyes hath laid
The wondrous clay from her own spittle made,
We see the widening ripples pass beyond,
The pond becomes the world, the world a pond,

All ether trembles when the pebble falls,
And a light word may ring in starry halls.
When first on earth the swift iambic ran
Men here and there were found but nowhere Man.
From whencesoe'er their origin they drew,
Each on its separate soil the species grew,
And by selection, natural or not,
Evolved a fond belief in one small spot.
The Greek himself, with all his wisdom, took
For the wide world his bright Aegean nook,
For fatherland, a town, for public, all
Who at one time could hear the herald bawl:
For him barbarians beyond his gate
Were lower beings, of a different date;
He never thought on such to spend his rhymes,
And if he did, they never read the *Times*.
Now all is changed, on this side and on that,
The Herald's learned to print and pass the hat;
His tone is so much raised that, far or near,
All with a sou to spend his news may hear, –
And who but, far or near, the sou affords
To learn the worst of foreigners and lords!
So comes the Pressman's heaven on earth, wherein
One touch of hatred proves the whole world kin –
'Our rulers are the best, and theirs the worst,
Our cause is always just and theirs accurst,
Our troops are heroes, hirelings theirs or slaves,
Our diplomats but children, theirs but knaves,
Our Press for independence justly prized,
Theirs bought or blind, inspired or subsidized.
For the world's progress what was ever made
Like to our tongue, our Empire and our trade?'
So chant the nations, till at last you'd think
Men could no nearer howl to folly's brink;
Yet some in England lately won renown
By howling word for word, but upside down.

But where, you cry, could poets find a place
(If poets we possessed) in this disgrace?
Mails will be mails, Reviews must be reviews,
But why the Critic with the Bard confuse?
Alas! Apollo, it must be confessed
Has lately gone the way of all the rest.
No more alone upon the far-off hills
With song serene the wilderness he fills,
But in the forum now his art employs
And what he lacks in knowledge gives in noise.
At first, ere he began to feel his feet,
He begged a corner in the hindmost sheet,
Concealed with Answers and Acrostics lay,
And held aloof from Questions of the Day.
But now, grown bold, he dashes to the front,
Among the leaders bears the battle's brunt,
Takes steel in hand, and cheaply unafraid
Spurs a lame Pegasus on Jameson's Raid,
Or pipes the fleet in melodrama's tones
To ram the Damned on their Infernal Thrones.

Sure, Scriblerus himself could scarce have guessed
The Art of Sinking might be further pressed:
But while these errors almost tragic loom
The Indian Drummer has but raised a boom.
'So well I love my country that the man
Who serves her can but serve her on my plan;
Be slim, be stalky, leave your Public Schools
To muffs like Bobs and other flannelled fools;
The lordliest life (since Buller made such hay)
Is killing men two thousand yards away;
You shoot the pheasant, but it costs too much
And does not tend to decimate the Dutch;
Your duty plainly then before you stands,
Conscription is the law for seagirt lands;
Prate not of freedom! Since I learned to shoot
I itch to use my ammunition boot.'

An odd way this, we thought, to criticize –
This barrackyard 'Attention! d— your eyes!'
But England smiled and lightly pardoned him,
For was he not her Mowgli and her Kim?
But now the neighbourhood remonstrance roars,
He's naughty still, and naughty out of doors.
'Tis well enough that he should tell Mamma
Her sons are tired of being what they are,
But to give friendly bears, expecting buns,
A paper full of stale unwholesome Huns –
One might be led to think, from all this work,
That little master's growing quite a Turk.

O Rudyard, Rudyard, in our hours of ease
(Before the war) you were not hard to please:
You loved a regiment whether fore or aft,
You loved a subaltern, however daft,
You loved the very dregs of barrack life,
The amorous Colonel and the sergeant's wife.
You sang the land where dawn across the Bay
Comes up to waken queens in Mandalay,
The land where comrades sleep by Cabul ford,
And Valour, brown or white, is Borderlord,
The secret Jungle-life of child and beast,
And all the magic of the dreaming East.
These, these we loved with you, and loved still more
The Seven Seas that break on Britain's shore,
The winds that know her labour and her pride,
And the Long Trail whereon our fathers died.

In that Day's Work be sure you gained, my friend,
If not the critic's name, at least his end;
Your song and story might have roused a slave
To see life bodily and see it brave.
With voice so genial and so long of reach
To your Own People you the Law could preach,

And even now and then without offence
To Lesser Breeds expose their lack of sense.
Return, return! and let us hear again
The ringing engines and the deep-sea rain,
The roaring chanty of the shore-wind's verse,
Too bluff to bicker and too strong to curse.
Let us again with hearts serene behold
The coastwise beacons that we knew of old;
So shall you guide us when the stars are veiled,
And stand among the Lights that never Failed.

Le Byron de nos Jours

or, The English Bar and Cross Reviewers

Still must I hear? – while Austin prints his verse
And Satan's sorrows fill Corelli's purse,
Must I not write lest haply some K.C.
To flatter Tennyson should sneer at me?
Or must the Angels of the Darker Ink
No longer tell the public what to think –
Must lectures and reviewing all be stayed
Until they're licensed by the Board of Trade?
Prepare for rhyme – I'll risk it – bite or bark
I'll stop the press for neither Gosse nor Clarke.

O sport most noble, when two cocks engage
With equal blindness and with equal rage!
When each, intent to pick the other's eye,
Sees not the feathers from himself that fly,
And, fired to scorch his rival's every bone,
Ignores the inward heat that grills his own;
Until self-plucked, self-spitted and self-roast,
Each to the other serves himself on toast.

But stay, but stay, you've pitched the key, my Muse,
A semi-tone too low for great Reviews;
Such penny whistling suits the cockpit's hum,
But here's a scene deserves the biggest drum.

Behold where high above the clamorous town
The vast Cathedral-towers in peace look down:
Hark to the entering crowd's incessant tread –
They bring their homage to the mighty dead.
Who in silk gown and fullest-bottomed wig
Approaches yonder, with emotion big?
Room for Sir Edward! now we shall be told
Which shrines are tin, which silver and which gold.
'Tis done! and now by life-long habit bound
He turns to prosecute the crowd around;
Indicts and pleads, sums up the *pro* and *con*,
The verdict finds and puts the black cap on.

'Prisoners, attend! of Queen Victoria's day
I am the Glory, you are the Decay.
You cannot think like Tennyson deceased,
You do not sing like Browning in the least.
Of Tennyson I sanction every word,
Browning I cut to something like one-third:
Though, mind you this, immoral he is not,
Still quite two-thirds I hope will be forgot.
He was to poetry a Tom Carlyle –
And that reminds me, Thomas too was vile.
He wrote a life or two, but parts, I'm sure,
Compared with other parts are very poor.
Now Dickens – most extraordinary – dealt
In fiction with what people really felt.
That proves his genius. Thackeray again
Is so unequal as to cause me pain.
And last of all, with History to conclude,
I've read Macaulay and I've heard of Froude.

114

That list, with all deductions, Gentlemen,
Will show that "now" is not the same as "then":
If you believe the plaintiff you'll declare
That English writers are not what they were.'

Down sits Sir Edward with a glowing breast,
And some applause is instantly suppressed.
Now up the nave of that majestic church
A quick uncertain step is heard to lurch.
Who is it? no one knows; but by his mien
He's the head verger, if he's not the Dean.

'What fellow's this that dares to treat us so?
This is no place for lawyers, out you go!
He is a brawler, Sir, who here presumes
To move our laurels and arrange our tombs.
Suppose that Meredith or Stephen said
(Or do you think those gentlemen are dead?)
This age has borne no advocates of rank,
Would not your face in turn be rather blank?
Come now, I beg you, go without a fuss,
And leave these high and heavenly things to us;
You may perhaps be some one, at the Bar,
But you are not in Orders, and we are.'

Sir Edward turns to go, but as he wends,
One swift irrelevant retort he sends.
'Your logic and your taste I both disdain,
You've quoted wrong from Jonson and Montaigne'.
The shaft goes home, and somewhere in the rear
Birrell in smallest print is heard to cheer.

And yet – and yet – conviction's not complete:
There was a time when Milton walked the street,
And Shakespeare singing in a tavern dark
Would not have much impressed Sir Edward Clarke.

To be alive – ay! there's the damning thing,
For who will buy a bird that's on the wing?
Catch, kill and stuff the creature, once for all,
And he may yet adorn Sir Edward's hall;
But while he's free to go his own wild way
He's not so safe as birds of yesterday.

In fine, if I must choose – although I see
That both are wrong – Great Gosse! I'd rather be
A critic suckled in an age outworn
Than a blind horse that starves knee-deep in corn.

Sailing at Dawn

One by one the pale stars die before the day now,
   One by one the great ships are stirring from their sleep,
Cables all are rumbling, anchors all a-weigh now,
   Now the fleet's a fleet again, gliding towards the deep.

   Now the fleet's a fleet again, bound upon the old ways,
      Splendour of the past comes shining in the spray;
   Admirals of old time, bring us on the bold ways!
      Souls of all the sea-dogs, lead the line to-day!

Far away behind us town and tower are dwindling,
   Home becomes a fair dream faded long ago;
Infinitely glorious the height of heaven is kindling,
   Infinitely desolate the shoreless sea below.

   Now the fleet's a fleet again, bound upon the old ways,
      Splendour of the past comes shining in the spray;
   Admirals of old time, bring us on the bold ways!
      Souls of all the sea-dogs, lead the line to-day!

Once again with proud hearts we make the old surrender,
  Once again with high hearts serve the age to be,
Not for us the warm life of Earth, secure and tender,
  Ours the eternal wandering and warfare of the sea.

Now the fleet's a fleet again, bound upon the old ways,
  Splendour of the past comes shining in the spray;
Admirals of old time, bring us on the bold ways!
  Souls of all the sea-dogs, lead the line to-day!

                 October 25th, 1909

The Song of the Sou'Wester

The sun was lost in a leaden sky,
  And the shore lay under our lee;
When a great Sou'Wester hurricane high
  Came rollicking up the sea.
He played with the fleet as a boy with boats
  Till out for the Downs we ran,
And he laugh'd with the roar of a thousand throats
  At the militant ways of man:

  Oh! I am the enemy most of might,
  The other be who you please!
  Gunner and guns may all be right,
  Flags a-flying and armour tight,
  But I am the fellow you've first to fight –
  The giant that swings the seas.

A dozen of middies were down below
  Chasing the X they love,
While the table curtseyed long and slow
  And the lamps were giddy above.

The lesson was all of a ship and a shot,
    And some of it may have been true,
But the word they heard and never forgot
    Was the word of the wind that blew:

Oh! I am the enemy most of might,
The other be who you please!
Gunner and guns may all be right,
Flags a-flying and armour tight,
But I am the fellow you've first to fight –
The giant that swings the seas.

The Middy with luck is a Captain soon,
    With luck he may hear one day
His own big guns a-humming the tune
    ' 'Twas in Trafalgar's Bay'.
But wherever he goes, with friends or foes,
    And whatever may there befall,
He'll hear for ever a voice he knows
    For ever defying them all:

Oh! I am the enemy most of might,
The other be who you please!
Gunner and guns may all be right,
Flags a-flying and armour tight,
But I am the fellow you've first to fight –
The giant that swings the seas.

November 30th, 1909

The Middle Watch

In a blue dusk the ship astern
   Uplifts her slender spars,
With golden lights that seem to burn
   Among the silver stars.
Like fleets along a cloudy shore
   The constellations creep,
Like planets on the ocean floor
   Our silent course we keep.

   And over the endless plain,
      Out of the night forlorn
   Rises a faint refrain,
      A song of the day to be born –
   Watch, oh watch till ye find again
      Life and the land of morn.

From a dim West to a dark East
   Our lines unwavering head,
As if their motion long had ceased
   And Time itself were dead.
Vainly we watch the deep below,
   Vainly the void above,
They died a thousand years ago –
   Life and the land we love.

   But over the endless plain,
      Out of the night forlorn
   Rises a faint refrain,
      A song of the day to be born –
   Watch, oh watch till ye find again
      Life and the land of morn.

December 19th, 1909

The Little Admiral

Stand by to reckon up your battleships –
    Ten, twenty, thirty, there they go.
Brag about your cruisers like Leviathans –
    A thousand men a-piece down below.
But here's just one little Admiral –
    We're all of us his brothers and his sons,
And he's worth, O he's worth at the very least
    Double all your tons and all your guns.

     Stand by, etc.

See them on the forebridge signalling –
    A score of men a-hauling hand to hand,
And the whole fleet flying like the wild geese
    Moved by some mysterious command.
Where's the mighty will that shows the way to them,
    The mind that sees ahead so quick and clear?
He's there, Sir, walking all alone there –
    The little man whose voice you never hear.

     Stand by, etc.

There are queer things that only come to sailormen;
    They're true, but they're never understood;
And I know one thing about the Admiral,
    That I can't tell rightly as I should.
I've been with him when hope sank under us –
    He hardly seemed a mortal like the rest,
I could swear that he had stars upon his uniform,
    And one sleeve pinned across his breast.

     Stand by, etc.

Some day we're bound to sight the enemy,
    He's coming, tho' he hasn't yet a name.
Keel to keel and gun to gun he'll challenge us
    To meet him at the Great Armada game.
None knows what may be the end of it,
    But we'll all give our bodies and our souls
To see the little Admiral a-playing him
    A rubber of the old Long Bowls!

    Stand by, etc.

January, 1910

The Song of the Guns at Sea

Oh hear! Oh hear!
Across the sullen tide,
Across the echoing dome horizon-wide
What pulse of fear
Beats with tremendous boom?
What call of instant doom,
With thunderstroke of terror and of pride,
With urgency that may not be denied,
Reverberates upon the heart's own drum —
Come!... Come!... for thou must come!

Come forth, O Soul!
This is thy day of power.
This is the day and this the glorious hour
That was the goal
Of thy self-conquering strife.
The love of child and wife,

The fields of Earth and the wide ways of Thought –
Did not thy purpose count them all as nought
That in this moment thou thyself mayst give
And in thy country's life for ever live?

Therefore rejoice
That in thy passionate prime
Youth's nobler hope disdained the spoils of Time
And thine own choice
Fore-earned for thee this day.
Rejoice! rejoice to obey
In the great hour of life that men call Death
The beat that bids thee draw heroic breath,
Deep-throbbing till thy mortal heart be dumb –
Come!... Come!... the time is come!

October, 1909

Farewell

Mother, with unbowed head
   Hear thou across the sea
The farewell of the dead,
   The dead who died for thee.
Greet them again with tender words and grave,
For, saving thee, themselves they could not save.

To keep the house unharmed
   Their fathers built so fair,
Deeming endurance armed
   Better than brute despair,
They found the secret of the word that saith,
'Service is sweet, for all true life is death'.

So greet thou well thy dead
   Across the homeless sea,
And be thou comforted
   Because they died for thee.
Far off they served, but now their deed is done
For evermore their life and thine are one.

January 18th, 1910

Mors Janua

Pilgrim, no shrine is here, no prison, no inn:
   Thy fear and thy belief alike are fond:
Death is a gate, and holds no room within:
   Pass – to the road beyond.

March 12th, 1910

Rilloby-Rill

Grasshoppers four a-fiddling went,
   Heigh-ho! never be still!
They earned but little towards their rent,
But all day long with their elbows bent
   They fiddled a tune called Rilloby-rilloby,
   Fiddled a tune called Rilloby-rill.

Grasshoppers soon on Fairies came,
   Heigh-ho! never be still!
Fairies asked with a manner of blame,
'Where do you come from, what is your name?
   What do you want with your Rilloby-rilloby,
   What do you want with your Rilloby-rill?'

'Madam, you see before you stand,
   Heigh-ho! never be still!
The Old Original Favourite Grand
Grasshopper's Green Herbarian Band,
   And the tune we play is Rilloby-rilloby,
   Madam, the tune is Rilloby-rill.'

Fairies hadn't a word to say,
   Heigh-ho! never be still!
Fairies seldom are sweet by day,
But the Grasshoppers merrily fiddled away,
   O but they played with a willoby-rilloby,
   O but they played with a willoby-will!

Fairies slumber and sulk at noon,
   Heigh-ho! never be still!
But at last the kind old motherly moon
Brought them dew in a silver spoon,
   And they turned to ask for Rilloby-rilloby,
   One more round of Rilloby-rill.

Ah! but nobody now replied,
   Heigh-ho! never be still!
When day went down the music died,
Grasshoppers four lay side by side,
   And there was an end of their Rilloby-rilloby,
   There was an end of their Rilloby-rill.

November 14th, 1909

124

To Belgium, 1914

The boast of legions, and the boast
   Of them that foster slaves for sons,
The triumph of the huger host,
   The vaunt of more gigantic guns –
These for an hour may fill the air
With cries of the primeval lair.

The fame of freedom and the fame
   Of them that dared deny the accurst,
The glory of the least in name,
   Who steeled their souls to battle first –
These are the crown of noble strife,
Man's hope and his enduring life.

The doom of heroes and the doom
   Of them who shed the innocent blood
Are sundered still in yonder tomb
   Beneath the all-enshrouding mud;
The scourge of earth in earth shall rot,
But faith shall live when fear is not.

July 2nd, 1918

A Ballad of Sir Pertab Singh

In the first year of him that first
   Was Emperor and King,
A rider came to the Rose-red House,
   The House of Pertab Singh.

Young he was and an Englishman,
   And a soldier, hilt and heel,
And he struck fire in Pertab's heart
   As the steel strikes on steel.

Beneath the morning stars they rode,
  Beneath the evening sun,
And their blood sang to them as they rode
  That all good wars are one.

They told their tales of the love of women,
  Their tales of East and West,
But their blood sang that of all their loves
  They loved a soldier best.

So ran their joy the allotted days,
  Till at the last day's end
The Shadow stilled the Rose-red House
  And the heart of Pertab's friend.

When morning came, in narrow chest
  The soldier's face they hid,
And over his fast-dreaming eyes
  Shut down the narrow lid.

Three were there of his race and creed,
  Three only and no more:
They could not find to bear the dead
  A fourth in all Jodhpore.

'O Maharaj, of your good grace
  Send us a Sweeper here:
A Sweeper has no caste to lose
  Even by an alien bier.'

'What need, what need?' said Pertab Singh,
  And bowed his princely head.
'I have no caste, for I myself
  Am bearing forth the dead.'

'O Maharaj, O passionate heart,
    Be wise, bethink you yet:
That which you lose to-day is lost
    Till the last sun shall set.'

'God only knows', said Pertab Singh,
    'That which I lose to-day:
And without me no hand of man
    Shall bear my friend away.'

Stately and slow and shoulder-high
    In the sight of all Jodhpore
The dead went down the rose-red steps
    Upheld by bearers four.

When dawn relit the lamp of grief
    Within the burning East
There came a word to Pertab Singh,
    The soft word of a priest.

He woke, and even as he woke
    He went forth all in white,
And saw the Brahmins bowing there
    In the hard morning light.

'Alas! O Maharaj, alas!
    O noble Pertab Singh!
For here in Jodhpore yesterday
    Befell a fearful thing.

'O here in Jodhpore yesterday
    A fearful thing befell.'
'A fearful thing', said Pertab Singh,
    'God and my heart know well –

'I lost a friend.'
                    'More fearful yet!
When down these steps you past
In sight of all Jodhpore you lost –
    O Maharaj! – your caste.'

Then leapt the light in Pertab's eyes
    As the flame leaps in smoke,
'Thou priest! thy soul hath never known
    The word thy lips have spoke.

'My caste! Know thou there is a caste
    Above my caste or thine,
Brahmin and Rajput are but dust
    To that immortal line:

'Wide as the world, free as the air,
    Pure as the pool of death –
The caste of all Earth's noble hearts
    Is the right soldier's faith.'

July 7th–8th, 1918

The War Films

O living pictures of the dead,
    O songs without a sound,
O fellowship whose phantom tread
    Hallows a phantom ground –
How in a gleam have these revealed
    The faith we had not found.

We have sought God in a cloudy Heaven,
   We have passed by God on earth:
His seven sins and his sorrows seven,
   His wayworn mood and mirth,
Like a ragged cloak have hid from us
   The secret of his birth.

Brother of men, when now I see
   The lads go forth in line,
Thou knowest my heart is hungry in me
   As for thy bread and wine:
Thou knowest my heart is bowed in me
   To take their death for mine.

October 8th, 1916

St George's Day

Ypres, 1915

To fill the gap, to bear the brunt
   With bayonet and with spade,
Four hundred to a four-mile front
   Unbacked and undismayed –
What men are these, of what great race,
   From what old shire or town,
That run with such goodwill to face
   Death on a Flemish down?

Let be! they bind a broken line.
   As men die, so die they.
Land of the free! their life was thine,
   It is St George's Day.

Yet say whose ardour bids them stand
   At bay by yonder bank,
Where a boy's voice and a boy's hand
   Close up the quivering rank,
Who under those all-shattering skies
   Plays out his captain's part
With the last darkness in his eyes
   And *Domum* in his heart?

Let be, let be! in yonder line
   All names are burned away.
Land of his love! the fame be thine,
   It is St George's Day.

January 5th, 1918

Hic Jacet

Qui in hoc saeculo fideliter militavit

He that has left hereunder
   The signs of his release
Feared not the battle's thunder
   Nor hoped that wars should cease;
No hatred set asunder
   His warfare from his peace.

Nor feared he in his sleeping
   To dream his work undone,
To hear the heathen sweeping
   Over the lands he won;
For he has left in keeping
   His sword unto his son.

August 12th, 1917

A Chanty of the Emden

The captain of the *Emden*
  He spread his wireless net,
And told the honest British tramp
  Where raiders might be met:
Where raiders might be met, my lads,
  And where the coast was clear,
And there he sat like a crafty cat
  And sang while they drew near –
    'Now you come along with me, sirs,
      You come along with me!
    You've had your run, old England's done,
      And it's time you were home from sea!'

The seamen of old England
  They doubted his intent,
And when he hailed, 'Abandon ship!'
  They asked him what he meant:
They asked him what he meant, my lads,
  The pirate and his crew,
But he said, 'Stand by! your ship must die,
  And it's luck you don't die too!
    So you come along with me, sirs,
      You come along with me:
    We find our fun now yours is done,
      And it's time you were home from sea!'

He took her, tramp or trader,
  He sank her like a rock,
He stole her coal and sent her down
  To Davy's deep-sea dock:
To Davy's deep-sea dock, my lads,
  The finest craft afloat,
And as she went he still would sing
  From the deck of his damned old boat –

'Now you come along with me, sirs,
      You come along with me:
   Your good ship's done with wind and sun,
      And it's time you were home from sea!'

The captain of the *Sydney*
   He got the word by chance;
Says he, 'By all the Southern Stars,
   We'll make the pirates dance:
We'll make the pirates dance, my lads,
   That this mad work have made,
For no man knows how a hornpipe goes
   Until the music's played.
      So you come along with me, sirs,
         You come along with me:
         The game's not won till the rubber's done,
            And it's time to be home from sea!'

The *Sydney* and the *Emden*
   They went it shovel and tongs,
The *Emden* had her rights to prove,
   The *Sydney* had her wrongs:
The *Sydney* had her wrongs, my lads,
   And a crew of South Sea blues;
Their hearts were hot, and as they shot
   They sang like kangaroos –
      'Now you come along with me, sirs,
         You come along with me:
         You've had your fun, you ruddy old Hun,
            And it's time you were home from sea!'

The *Sydney* she was straddled,
   But the *Emden* she was strafed,
They knocked her guns and funnels out,
   They fired her fore and aft:

They fired her fore and aft, my lads,
  And while the beggar burned
They salved her crew to a tune they knew,
  But never had rightly learned –
    'Now you come along with me, sirs,
      You come along with me:
    We'll find you fun till the fighting's done
      And the pirate's off the sea –
    Till the pirate's off the sea, my lads,
      Till the pirate's off the sea:
    We'll find them fun till the fighting's done
      And the pirate's off the sea!'

January 13th, 1918

The Toy Band

A SONG OF THE GREAT RETREAT

Dreary lay the long road, dreary lay the town,
  Lights out and never a glint o' moon:
Weary lay the stragglers, half a thousand down,
  Sad sighed the weary big Dragoon.
'Oh! if I'd a drum here to make them take the road again,
  'Oh! if I'd a fife to wheedle, Come, boys, come!
You that mean to fight it out, wake and take your load again,
  Fall in! Fall in! Follow the fife and drum!

'Hey, but here's a toy shop, here's a drum for me,
  Penny whistles too to play the tune!
Half a thousand dead men soon shall hear and see
  We're a band!' said the weary big Dragoon.
'Rubadub! Rubadub! Wake and take the road again,
  Wheedle-deedle-deedle-dee, Come, boys, come!
You that mean to fight it out, wake and take your load again,
  Fall in! Fall in! Follow the fife and drum!'

133

Cheerly goes the dark road, cheerly goes the night,
　　Cheerly goes the blood to keep the beat:
Half a thousand dead men marching on to fight
　　With a little penny drum to lift their feet.
Rubadub! Rubadub! Wake and take the road again,
　　Wheedle-deedle-deedle-dee, Come, boys, come!
You that mean to fight it out, wake and take your load again,
　　Fall in! Fall in! Follow the fife and drum!

As long as there's an Englishman to ask a tale of me,
　　As long as I can tell the tale aright,
We'll not forget the penny whistle's wheedle-deedle-dee
　　And the big Dragoon a-beating down the night,
Rubadub! Rubadub! Wake and take the road again,
　　Wheedle-deedle-deedle-dee, Come, boys, come!
You that mean to fight it out, wake and take your load again,
　　Fall in! Fall in! Follow the fife and drum!

December 14th, 1914

A Letter from the Front

I was out early to-day, spying about
From the top of a haystack – such a lovely morning –
And when I mounted again to canter back
I saw across a field in the broad sunlight
A young gunner subaltern, stalking along
With a rook-rifle held at the ready and – would you believe it? –
A domestic cat, soberly marching behind him.

So I laughed, and felt quite well-disposed to the youngster,
And shouted out 'The top of the morning' to him,
And wished him 'Good sport!' – and then I remembered
My rank, and his, and what I ought to be doing;

And I rode nearer, and added, 'I can only suppose
You have not seen the Commander-in-Chief's orders
Forbidding English officers to annoy their Allies
By hunting and shooting.'
                     But he stood and saluted
And said earnestly, 'I beg your pardon, sir,
I was only going out to shoot a sparrow
To feed my cat with.'

                 So there was the whole picture –
The lovely early morning, the occasional shell
Screeching and scattering past us, the empty landscape –
Empty, except for the young gunner saluting
And the cat, anxiously watching his every movement.

I may be wrong, and I may have told it badly,
But it struck *me* as being extremely ludicrous.

1915

The Great Memory

Nobis cum pereant amorum
Et dulcedines et decor,
Tu nostrorum praeteritorum,
Anima mundi, sis memor.

On the mind's lonely hill-top lying
   I saw man's life go by like a breath,
And Love that longs to be love undying,
   Bowed with fear of the void of death.
'If Time be master', I heard her weeping,
   'How shall I save the loves I bore?
They are gone, they are gone beyond my keeping –
   Anima mundi, sis memor!

135

'Soul of the World, thou seest them failing –
   Childhood's loveliness, child's delight –
Lost as stars in the daylight paling,
   Trodden to earth as flowers in fight.
Surely in these thou hast thy pleasure –
   Yea! they are thine and born therefor:
Shall they not be with thy hid treasure? –
   Anima mundi, sis memor!

'Only a moment we can fold them
   Here in the home whose life they are:
Only a moment more behold them
   As in a picture, small and far.
Oh, in the years when even this seeming
   Lightens the eyes of Love no more,
Dream them still in thy timeless dreaming
   Anima mundi, sis memor!'

September 7th–8th, 1919

March 5th, 1921

Me at the dawn's first breath
Thee in the dusk of death
   Thy love and my love tended:
We shall be mother and son
After all days are done
   All darkness ended.

March, 1921

A Perpetual Memory

GOOD FRIDAY, 1915

Broken and pierced, hung on the bitter wire,
   By their most precious death the Sons of Man
Redeem for us the life of our desire –
   O Christ how often since the world began!

The Linnet's Nest

O what has wrought again the miracle of Spring?
This old garden of mine that was so beautiful
And died so utterly – what power of earth or sky
From dead sticks and dead mould has raised up Paradise?

The flow'rs we knew we welcome again in their turns–
Primrose, anemone, daffodil and tulip,
Blossom of cherry, blossom of pear and apple,
Iris and columbine, and now the white cistus.

In a round bush it grows, this cistus of delight,
A mound of delicate pure white crinkled petals,
In the heart of the garden, where the green paths cross,
Where the old stone dial throws its morning shadow.

Come nearer, and speak low; watch while I put aside
This thickly flow'ring spray, and stoop till you can see
There in the shadowy centre, a tiny nest,
And on it, facing us, a bright-eyed bird sitting.

She has five eggs, shaped and speckled most daintily;
But this she cannot know, nor how they are quick'ning
With that which soon will be on the wing, and singing
The ancestral linnet-song of thoughtless rapture.

No, this she cannot know, nor indeed anything
That we call knowledge, nor such love and hope as ours:
Yet she for her treasure will endure and tremble,
And so find peace that passeth our understanding.

You wonder at my wonder – the bird has instinct,
The law by dust ordained for that which dust creates?
What then is beauty? and love? my heart is restless
To know what love and beauty are worth in the end.

The bird I know will fly; nest, brood, cistus, garden
Will all be lost when winter takes the world again:
Yet in my mind their loveliness will still survive
Till I too in my turn obey the laws of dust.

Are we then all? Is there no Life in whom our nests,
Our trembling hopes and our unintelligent loves
May still, for the beauty they had, the faith they kept,
Live on as in a vast eternal memory?

Yet so for us would beauty still be meaningless,
Mortal and meaningless – our hearts are restless still
To be one with that spirit from whom all life springs,
And therein to behold all beauty for ever.

Perhaps the linnet too is more than dust: perhaps
She, though so small, of so quick-perishing beauty,
Is none the less a part of His immortal dream
And beneath her breast cherishes the divine life.

May 17th, 1924

The Nightjar

We loved our Nightjar, but she would not stay with us.
We had found her lying as dead, but soft and warm,
Under the apple tree beside the old thatched wall.
Two days we kept her in a basket by the fire,
Fed her, and thought she well might live – till suddenly
In the very moment of most confiding hope
She raised herself all tense, quivered and drooped and died.
Tears sprang into my eyes – why not? the heart of man
Soon sets itself to love a living companion,
The more so if by chance it asks some care of him.
And this one had the kind of loveliness that goes
Far deeper than the optic nerve – full fathom five
To the soul's ocean cave, where Wonder and Reason
Tell their alternate dreams of how the world was made.
So wonderful she was – her wings the wings of night
But powdered here and there with tiny golden clouds
And wave-line markings like sea-ripples on the sand.
O how I wish I might never forget that bird –
Never!
        But even now, like all beauty of earth,
She is fading from me into the dusk of Time.

May, 1925

The Star in the West

Listen with me tonight, listen O tenderly
To the wordless wailing of yonder newborn Child.
In vain his mother's arms enfold him and soothe him,
In vain her voice murmurs the song of tireless love.

Why does he weep? Why will he not be comforted?
Here on the threshold of his life, what does he dread?
Is it the dimness of the stable where he lies,
Or the gaunt ox and ass, shadows of toil to come?

Presently will he not uplift his wond'ring eyes
To see the face that is to be his earthly rest?
Will not the shining star above his low roof stayed
Lighten his childish dream with serene rays of peace?

Dare not to ask! – unless ye dare also to hear
The story of his cross, his first and second death –
That men have murdered Night, and made stars of their own,
And flung them down from heav'n, and Peace has died by fire.

November, 1932

Paradiso xxxiii, 58

Qual è colui che somniando vede
    che dopo il sogno la passione impressa
    rimane, e l'altro alla mente non riede:

Cotal son io, che quasi tutta cessa
    mia visione, ed ancor mi distilla
    nel cor lo dolce che nacque da essa.

As he who sees in dream, and when the dream is past
    the passion stamped upon his being still remains
    although the dream itself come no more to the mind;

Such am I now, for almost wholly gone from me
    is that my vision, yet still falling drop by drop
    within my heart remains the sweetness born of it.

Sulpicia's Confession

Light of mine eyes, if this be not the truth
   Never may I be near thy heart again:
Of all the faults of all my foolish youth
   Not one has brought me such remorseful pain
As that last night I let thee sleep alone,
   And starved thy passion but to hide my own.

A Letter to R. B. after a Visit

AUGUST, 1921

Written in his host's 'New narrative method'

My dear Bridges before I do anything else
I must thank you for my visit: it was all good –
From the kind welcome and renewal of friendship
Down to that excellent wine and Devonshire cream.
I believe I did say something of my feelings,
But words are useless: I might go on heaping them
Epithet on epithet all down my paper
Like the elephant piling teak in Kipling's poem
And still leave the real thing wholly unexpressed.
But I do wish I could give you some idea
Of how much I like your new narrative method
And admire the poems by which you shew it off,
Especially of course the polyglot parrot
Who demonstrates in a ludicrous but apt image
How you in verse whose service is perfect freedom
Can tell a plain prosy tale, or write a letter,
Or toss a song to the stars or the salt seawind,
Or toll the deep old Latin and Italian bells,
Or dance among French accents without breaking them
Or wake again the poignant memories of Greece.

But here is post time, and this must go.

Believe me

My dear Bridges (how glad I am to write the words)
If you are my 'old friend', as your kindness declared,
I am yours too, as always grateful and devoted.

H. N.
September 1st, 1921

To E. C.

Rivers when beheld afar
Often blue and golden are;
Nearer seen the shining flood
Turns to sluggish tides of mud.

Dearest, when to you I seem
Such a dull unlovely stream,
Read, and think that even I
Can at times reflect the sky.

For a War Memorial

CLIFTON COLLEGE, 1914–1918

From the Great Marshal to the last recruit
  These Clifton, were thyself, thy spirit in deed,
Thy flower of chivalry, thy fallen fruit
  And thine immortal seed.

Notes, by Henry Newbolt

San Stefano, *page 33*

Sir Peter Parker was the son of Admiral Christopher Parker, grandson of Admiral Sir Peter Parker (the life-long friend and chief mourner of Nelson) and great-grandson of Admiral Sir William Parker. On his mother's side he was grandson of Admiral Byron, and first cousin of Lord Byron, the poet. He was killed in action near Baltimore in 1814, and buried in St Margaret's, Westminster, where may be seen the monument erected to his memory by the officers of the *Menelaus*.

Drake's Drum, *page 35*

A State drum, painted with the arms of Sir Francis Drake, is preserved among other relics at Buckland Abbey, the seat of the Drake family in Devon.

The Fighting Téméraire, *page 36*

The last two stanzas have been misunderstood. It seems, therefore, necessary to state that they are intended to refer to Turner's picture in the National Gallery of 'The Fighting *Téméraire* tugged to her Last Berth'.

The Quarter-Gunner's Yarn, *page 49*

This ballad is founded on fragmentary lines communicated to the author by Admiral Sir Windham Hornby, K.C.B., who served under Sir Thomas Hardy in 1827. For an account of Cheeks the Marine see Marryat's *Peter Simple*.

Seringapatam, *page 57*

In 1780, while attempting to relieve Arcot, a British force of three thousand men was cut to pieces by Hyder Ali. Baird, then a young captain in the 73rd, was left for dead on the field. He was afterwards, with forty-nine other officers, kept in prison at Seringapatam, and treated with Oriental barbarity and treachery by Hyder Ali and his son Tippoo Sahib, Sultans of Mysore. Twenty-three of the prisoners died by poison, torture, and fever; the rest were surrendered in 1784. In 1799, at the Siege of Seringapatam, Major-General Baird commanded the first European brigade, and volunteered to lead the storming column. Tippoo Sahib, with eight thousand of his men, fell in the assault, but the victor spared the lives of his sons, and forbade a general sack of the city.

Clifton Chapel, *pages 63 and 142*

Thirty-five Old Cliftonian Officers served in the campaign of 1897 on the Indian Frontier, of whom twenty-two were mentioned in despatches, and six recommended for the Distinguished Service Order. Of the three hundred Cliftonians who served in the war in South Africa, thirty were killed in action and fourteen died of wounds or fever.

More than 3,000 have served in the Great War, of whom over 500 have been killed in four years. Their honours are past count.

On Spion Kop, *page 78*

Major N. H. Vertue, of the Buffs, Brigade-Major to General Woodgate, was buried where he fell, on the edge of Spion Kop, in front of the British position.

Sráhmandázi, *page 82*

This ballad is founded on materials given to the author by the late Miss Mary Kingsley on her return from her last visit to the Bantu peoples of West Africa. The songnet, as described by her, resembles a long piece of fishing-net folded, and is carried by the Songman over his shoulder. When opened and laid before an audience, it is seen to contain 'tokens' – such as a leopard's paw, a child's hair, a necklet, or a dried fish – sewn firmly to the meshes of the net. These form a kind of symbolical index to the Songman's repertory; the audience make their choice by laying a hand upon any token which appears desirable. The last of the tokens is that which represents the Song of Dying, or Song of Sráhmandázi. It is a shapeless piece of any substance, and is recognised only by its position in the net. The song, being unintelligible to the living, is never asked for until the moment of death.

Rondel, *page 87*

This and the two following pieces are from the French of Wenceslas, Duke of Brabant and Luxembourg, who died in 1384.

Epistle to Colonel Francis Edward Younghusband, *page 98*

Lines 19–21. In the school quadrangle at Clifton, the site from which, upon occasion, the grandstand used to overlook the Close is now occupied by the Memorial to those Cliftonians who fell in the South African War.

Le Byron de nos Jours, *page 113*

This parody, which first appeared in *The Monthly Review*, was an attempt to sum up and commemorate a literary discussion of the day. On Saturday night, 15 November, 1902, at the Working Men's College, Great Ormond Street, Sir Edward Clarke, K.C., delivered an address on 'The Glory and Decay of English Literature in the Reign of Victoria'. Sir Edward, who mentioned incidentally that he lectured at the college forty years ago, said that there was a rise from the beginning of that reign to the period 1850–60, and that from the latter date there had been a very strange and lamentable decline to the end of the reign, would, he thought, be amply demonstrated. A glorious galaxy of talent adorned the years 1850–60. There were two great poets, two great novelists, and two great historians. The two great poets were Alfred Tennyson and Robert Browning. The first named would always stand at the head of the literature of the Victorian period. There was no poet in the whole course of our history whose works were more likely to live as a complete whole than his, and there was not a line which his friends would wish to see blotted out. Robert Browning was a poet of strange inequality and of extraordinary and fantastic methods in his composition. However much one could enjoy some of his works, one could only hope that two-thirds of them would be as promptly as possible forgotten – not, however, from any moral objection to what he wrote. He was the Carlyle of poetry. By his Lives of Schiller and Sterling, Carlyle showed that he *could* write beautiful and pure English, but that he should descend to the style of some of his later works was a melancholy example of misdirected energy. . . . Charles Dickens was perhaps the most extraordinary genius of those who had endeavoured to deal with fiction as illustrative of the actual experiences of life. With Dickens there stood the great figure of Thackeray, who had left a great collection of books, very unequal in their quality, but containing amongst them some of the finest things ever written in the English tongue. The two great historians were Macaulay and Froude. To-day we had no great novelists. Would anyone suggest we had a poet? (Laughter). After the year 1860 there were two great names in poetry – the two Rosettis. There had been no book produced in the last ten years which could compete with any one of the books produced from 1850 to 1860.

To this Mr Edmund Gosse replied a week later at the Dinner of the *Encyclopaedia Britannica*. He reminded his audience that even the most perspicuous people in past times had made the grossest blunders when they judged their own age. Let them remember the insensibility of Montaigne to the merits of all his contemporaries. In the next age, and in their own country, Ben Jonson took occasion at the very moment when Shakespeare was producing his masterpieces, to lament the total decay of poetry in England. We could not see the trees for the wood behind them, but we ought to be confident they were growing all the time.

Mr Gosse also wrote to *The Times* on behalf of 'the Profession' of Letters, reminding Sir Edward of the names of Swinburne and William Morris, Hardy and Stevenson, Creighton and Gardiner, and asking what would be the feelings of the learned gentleman if Meredith or Leslie Stephen (of whose existence he was perhaps unaware) should put the question in public, 'Would anyone suggest we have an Advocate?'

Sir Edward, in his rejoinder, had no difficulty in showing that Mr Gosse's citation of Montaigne and Jonson was not verbally exact. Mr Birrell added some comments which were distinguished by being printed in type of a markedly different size.

To the author of these lines, the controversy appears so typical and so likely to arise again, that he desires to record, in however slight a form, his recollection of it, and his own personal bias, which is in no degree lessened by reconsideration after several years.

Further Notes, by Patric Dickinson

Drake's Drum, *page 35*
The circumstances of the appearance of this poem are remarkable. In January 1896 Kaiser Wilhelm made 'a threatening move' at sea. A Special Service Squadron of the Royal Navy put to sea at a moment's notice ready to fight if necessary. In this ominous atmosphere Newbolt felt that a poem he had written in the previous month would be appropriate and sent it to Sidney Low, Editor of the *St James's Gazette*. It appeared on January 15th and entirely caught the public mood. Low, without consulting Newbolt, reversed the order of verses one and two, and 'corrected' some of the dialect spelling.

Vitaï Lampada, *page 38*
The earliest written of Newbolt's published poems.

A Ballad of John Nicholson, *page 39*
John Nicholson (1821–57) was mortally wounded and died at the siege of Delhi. It is clear that he was already regarded as an outstanding soldier with great qualities of valour, integrity and personality. 'One of the great men' of the Mutiny period – the other being Sir Arthur Lawrence. Had he lived, Queen Victoria would have made him K.C.B.

Ionicus, *page 44*
Ionicus is the poet William Cory (formerly Johnson), 1823–92, who is known for his two anthology pieces *Heraclitus* and *Mimnermus in church*. He was a keen patriot who would break off his teaching at Eton if soldiers were marching by and take his class out to see them . . . 'his life a tangle seemed' is an oblique reference to the homosexuality for which he was sacked.
Sir Denis Pack (1772–1823) was an Irish career soldier who distinguished himself in the Peninsular war and commanded a brigade of Picton's division at Quatre Bras and Waterloo. Sir Thomas Picton (1758–1815), a Welshman, had a long and successful military career in the West Indies and also in Spain. He came out of retirement when

147

he heard of Napoleon's escape from Elba, and his last words at Waterloo were 'Charge! Charge! Hurrah!' He was then struck dead by a cannon ball on the head.

Minora Sidera, *page 45*

The D.N.B. was then being compiled under the editorship of Newbolt's great friend Sir Leslie Stephen. Most of Newbolt's military heroes led lives 'obscurely great' which are chronicled in it.

The Vigil, *page 47*

From a letter, August 8th, 1914 '. . . "*The Vigil*" is being quoted, sung, recited and reprinted from one end of the country to the other . . . but so far no-one – even among my friends – has observed that it was published in 1898 and has appeared in all three of my published volumes since then.'

Admiral Death, *page 48*

Newbolt sat for William Strang, the painter and etcher, (1859–1921) in 1898. 'While I sat to him he had set up an oil painting for me to fix my eyes upon – it was a Holbeinesque thing, with a jigging skeleton in it, and he said as he drew me, "You should do a ballad on Death – Admiral Death."' Strang couldn't explain to Newbolt what he meant, '. . . but afterwards – in less than a week – the ballad came to me suddenly and easily with a meaning of its own.'

Craven, *page 51*

Newbolt's heroes were often almost contemporary. Craven's daughters wrote to him from America to tell him that this was truly the kind of man their father all his life was. Lucas, an earlier hero (see '*Seringapatam*'), is of the same personal-to-Newbolt category.

Sir James Outram (1803–63) was however a soldier and administrator known throughout India. 'Gentlemen, I give you the "Bayard of India", sans peur et sans reproche' was a toast to him in 1842. 'A fox is a fool and a lion is a coward compared with James Outram', is another contemporary judgement. The Chevalier de Bayard was the exemplar of all the knightly qualities of the middle ages. Pious, modest, humane and fearless – a man to whom the greatest of virtues was justice.

Gillespie, *page 55*

Sir Robert Rollo Gillespie (1766–1814) was by no means a 'parfit gentil knight' and the account of his life makes variegated reading.

What is remarkable about this exploit is that he was forty when, on July 10th, 1806, he accomplished it. From Arcot to Vellore is fourteen miles.

Seringapatam, *page 57*
Sir David Baird (1757–1829). The idea of the soldier and administrator being sans peur et sans reproche must have been strong for a pun on Sir David's name, 'not Baird but Bayard' (see Outram) was current in India. He is also remembered as the victor of Pondicherry and for his part in the Peninsular war, his final engagement being the withdrawal on Corunna.

He Fell among Thieves, *page 61*
Newbolt was usually at great pains in his ballads to get his facts right. This famous poem is an instance of his idealising and perhaps identifying himself with his hero. Lieutenant George W. Hayward was indeed done to death 'after he had left Yasin for the Pamirs in July 1870', but the circumstances were rather different. In 1918 Newbolt was dining next to the ex-Viceroy Lord Curzon of Kedleston, who spoke of the poem and afterwards found out the facts about Hayward as far as possible. 'You speak of him as apparently having had a University education – "College Eights", "Dons", etc. I dare say I could find this out [too] but I should have thought it unlikely in the case of a young Lieutenant fifty years ago . . .' Newbolt based the poem on an account of Hayward's death as told in the Younghusbands' *Chitral*.

The Non-Combatant, *page 63*
Newbolt was so incensed by an attack on *Admirals All* in the *Athenaeum*, which said that patriotic poetry was an impossibility, 'rhetoric mistaken for poetry', that he wrote and tore up furious letters to the Editor, finally sent one, and then asked that this poem might be substituted, which it was.

Moonset, *page 72*
Seven o'clock on a dark January morning, en route from Orchard-leigh to Bamburgh. 'An hour or two of my day's journey was spent in "recollecting in tranquillity" this strange experience of "Moonset".'

Peace, *page 80*
This quatrain was prompted by Virginia Stephen (Woolf). . . . 'I remember too that when the time came for making peace one of his

[Leslie Stephen's] daughters made a comment which stirred my sympathetic emotion . . .' (1902)

Dear Mr Newbolt,

You must have been good enough to send me a postcard with a little poem on it which gives me great pleasure – and pride. I have spent Sunday at a home where the only book is your *Admirals All*, and now I come back to find this. Father is rehearsing 'Drake's Drum' for Wednesday. Thank you very much.

Yours very sincerely,
Virginia Stephen.

Yattendon, *page 90*

This is the village in Berkshire where Robert Bridges lived. The poem is obscure unless it is realised that he is the singer to whom the 'pilgrim world must come'.

The Old Superb, *page 95*

Listening to a recording of this in 1929 Newbolt wrote: 'I was quite overcome with admiration of old Charles Stanford's genius . . . I had only one thing to say, and that a quotation – 'What genius we had in those days! I wrote that "Old Superb" in one piece and next day he set it in one morning. Could one enjoy life more gloriously?'

Ave, Soror, *page 104*

' . . . it was in the Hursley Copse [near Winchester] that my youth came back to me for a moment and I called to my little daughter, who had strayed from us in the underwood, by the name of my sister, long since irrecoverably lost.'

Fond Counsel, *page 107*

These lines were specially written for H. Walford Davies to set to music.

Songs of the Fleet, *pages 116–122*

These six poems recollect Newbolt's week at sea as guest of Admiral Sir Reginald Custance, in command of the Channel fleet, in May 1908. Five of them (not 'The Song of the Guns at Sea') were set to music by Sir Charles Stanford and first published in that form (Boosey & Co, Stainer & Bell, 1910). This group of songs is sometimes confused with *Songs of the Sea* (Boosey & Co, 1904). These more popular settings, also by Stanford, are of 'Drake's Drum', 'Outward Bound', 'Waggon Hill' (under the title 'Devon, O Devon'), 'Homeward Bound', and 'The Old Superb'.

A Ballad of Sir Pertab Singh, *page 125*
As in other ballads, Newbolt was often inspired by written accounts or by stories: '(15 January 1918) Dunlop Smith told me this story last night. I never heard one that pleased me more. It ought to make a pair for John Nicholson.'

The War Films, *page 128*
'The "Somme film" . . . If only I could get that desire for fellowship into a few verses, it would be a new poem or an immortal one.' In this letter to Lady Alice Hylton (September 16, 1916) Newbolt expatiates on comradeship and 'the love of man in the mass that we always admit to be a main part of Christianity, but never feel ourselves.'

St George's Day, *page 129*
A poem at once public, and intensely private. It was symbolically upon St George's Day that the poet's son Francis went into action (and was wounded) near Ypres. He survived the war.

The Toy Band, *page 133*
Major-General Sir Tom Bridges (1871–1939). Tom Bridges was Robert Bridges' nephew. This valorous exploit took place at St Quentin, August 27th, 1914. It was known to the Prime Minister, Herbert Asquith. 'He's one of the heroes of the war – there are three heroes – French, and Haig, and Bridges', he said to Newbolt in December. The poem appeared in *The Times* for December 16th.

For a War Memorial, *page 142*
The Great Marshal is Field-Marshal Earl Haig who was at Clifton.

Index of Titles

Index of First Lines

I cannot tell, of twain beneath this bond, 88
I left behind the ways of care, 104
I sat by the granite pillar, and sunlight fell, 81
I was out early to-day, spying about, 134
In a blue dusk the ship astern, 119
In seventeen hundred and fifty nine, 37
In the first year of him that first, 125
It fell in the year of Mutiny, 39
It was eight bells ringing, 36
It was morning at St Helen's, in the great and gallant days, 33
It's good to see the School we knew, 92

Lad, and can you rest now, 97
Laden with spoil of the South, fulfilled with the glory of achieve-
    ment, 54
Ladies, where were your bright eyes glancing, 68
Let others praise, as fancy wills, 46
Light of mine eyes, if this be not the truth, 141
Listen with me tonight, listen O tenderly, 139
Long ago to thee I gave, 88
Lover of England, stand awhile and gaze, 51

Me at the dawn's first breath, 136
Memories long in music sleeping, 67
Mother, with unbowed head, 122
My dear Bridges before I do anything else, 141

No more to watch by Night's eternal shore, 80

O bitter wind toward the sunset blowing, 76
O living pictures of the dead, 128
O Lord Almighty, Thou whose hands, 73
O Saint whose thousand shrines our feet have trod, 85
O son of mine, when dusk shall find thee bending, 86
O what has wrought again the miracle of Spring?, 137
O Youth, beside thy silver-springing fountain, 107
Oh hear! Oh hear!, 121
On the mind's lonely hill-top lying, 135
One by one the pale stars die before the day now, 116
One day, when Love and Summer both were young, 106

Our game was his but yesteryear, 78
Over the downs in sunlight clear, 108
Over the turret, shut in his iron-clad tower, 51

Past seven o'clock: time to be gone, 72
Pilgrim, no shrine is here, no prison, no inn, 123

Riding at dawn, riding alone, 55
Rivers when beheld afar, 142

She is a lady fair and wise, 90
She's the daughter of the breeze, 93
Since thou and I have wandered from the highway, 105
Sitting at times over a hearth that burns, 45
Sons of the Island Race, wherever ye dwell, 42
Spring, they say, with his greenery, 70
Stand by to reckon up your battleships, 120
Still must I hear? – while Austin prints his verse, 113

The boast of legions, and the boast, 125
The captain of the *Emden*, 131
'The sleep that Tippoo Sahib sleeps, 57
The Squire sat propped in a pillowed chair, 64
The stars were faint in heaven, 102
The sun was lost in a leaden sky, 117
The wind was rising easterly, the morning sky was blue, 95
There's a breathless hush in the Close to-night, 38
They saw the cables loosened, they saw the gangways cleared, 74
This is the Chapel: here, my son, 63
Though I wander far-off ways, 87
'Tis hard to say if greater waste of time, 109
To fill the gap, to bear the brunt, 129
To Youth there comes a whisper out of the west, 108
To-day, my friend is seventy-five, 69
Turn back, my Soul, no longer set, 105

Walking to-day in your garden, O gracious lady, 103
We lay at St Helen's, and easy she rode, 49
We loved our Nightjar, but she would not stay with us, 139
When England sets her banner forth, 94